Grammar Rules!

Tanya Gibb

NSW Edition

Name: ________________________________

Class: ________________________________

Grammar Rules! Student Book 2
NSW Edition
ISBN: 978 0 6550 9242 1

Publisher: Catherine Charles-Brown
Designer and typesetter: Trish Hayes
Illustrator: Stephen Michael King
Series editor: Marie James
Indigenous consultant: Al Fricker

This edition published in 2023 by Matilda Education Australia, an imprint of Meanwhile Education Pty Ltd
Melbourne, Australia
T: 1300 277 235
E: customersupport@matildaed.com.au
www.matildaeducation.com.au

First edition published in 2008 by Macmillan Science and Education Australia Pty Ltd

Publication data
Author: Tanya Gibb
Title: *Grammar Rules! Student Book 2 NSW Edition*
ISBN: 978 0 6550 9242 1

A catalogue record for this book is available from the National Library of Australia

Printed in China by Central
Sep-2022

Contents

Note to Teachers and Parents

Grammar Rules!

Grammar Rules! comprehensively meets the requirements of the 2021 NSW Education Standards Authority **English K–2 Syllabus**, which states that "through practice and experience in understanding and creating texts, students learn about the power, purpose, value and art of English for communication, knowledge and enjoyment" (p15). *Grammar Rules!* also supports implementation of **Australian Curriculum English**, V9, 2022.

The **NSW English K–2 Syllabus** recognises that knowledge and understanding of grammar at the level of the whole text and at the level of the sentence, clause, phrase or word, underpins students' comprehension of oral and written texts, and their ability to create effective texts for various purposes and audiences.

Grammar Rules! provides a conceptually sound, scope and sequence of context-based activities that support teaching and learning in English. Although the title for the series is *Grammar Rules!*, the series in not just about grammar. Each unit of work in the series begins at the level of the whole text by identifying purpose and audience for the model text, providing teaching opportunities to activate students' background knowledge of the topic or the text type, and then supporting students in reading comprehension. The texts provided can be used for discussion of text forms and features and sentence structures, as well as for vocabulary expansion. The texts can also be used as models for students to use when creating their own written, spoken or multimodal texts. The texts included in *Grammar Rules!* cover a variety of informative, imaginative and persuasive texts and hybrid texts that use elements of different types of texts.

Grammar Rules! also teaches the conventions of punctuation and some aspects of spelling (for example, plural nouns, suffixes and prefixes); literary elements such as onomatopoeia, rhyme and alliteration; and the way visual elements function to support or construct meaning. Other areas of the **English K–2 Syllabus** covered in *Grammar Rules!* include critical reading and reflecting on character, setting and plot in narrative texts (literature).

Student Book 2

Units of work

Student Book 2 contains 35 weekly units of work presented in a conceptually sound scope and sequence. The intention is for students to work through the units in the sequence in which they are presented. See the **Scope and Sequence Chart** on pages 6–7 for more information. There are also regular Revision Units that can be used for consolidation or assessment purposes.

The sample texts in *Student Book 2* are not tied to any particular content across other curriculum areas. This allows teachers and students to focus on the way language is structured in the different types of texts according to purpose and audience. Students can then use this knowledge to critically evaluate, respond to and create texts in other learning areas.

Icons

Encourages students to create texts of their own to demonstrate their understanding of the text structures and features taught in the unit. These activities focus on written language; however, many also provide opportunities for using spoken language to engage with others, make presentations and develop skills in using ICT.

Highlights useful grammatical rules and concepts. The rule is always introduced the first time students need it to complete an activity.

Tells students that a special hint is provided for an activity. It might be a tip about language functions, or a reminder to look at a rule in a previous unit.

Encourages students to assess their progress across each unit.

Grammar Rules! Glossary

A valuable glossary is provided at the end of *Student Book 2*. Teachers and students can use this as a straightforward dictionary of grammar terminology, or as a summary of important grammar rules used in *Student Book 2*. Page references are also given for the point in the book where the rule was first introduced, so that students can go back to that unit if they need more information or further revision of the rule.

Grammar Rules! Student Book 2 (ISBN 9780655092421) © Tanya Gibb/Matilda Education Australia

Pull-Out Writing Log

At the centre of *Student Book 2* is a practical pull-out Writing Log so that students can keep track of the texts they have created or attempted to create. The Writing Log also includes a handy reminder of the writing process, as well as a checklist of types of texts for students to try.

Unit At A Glance

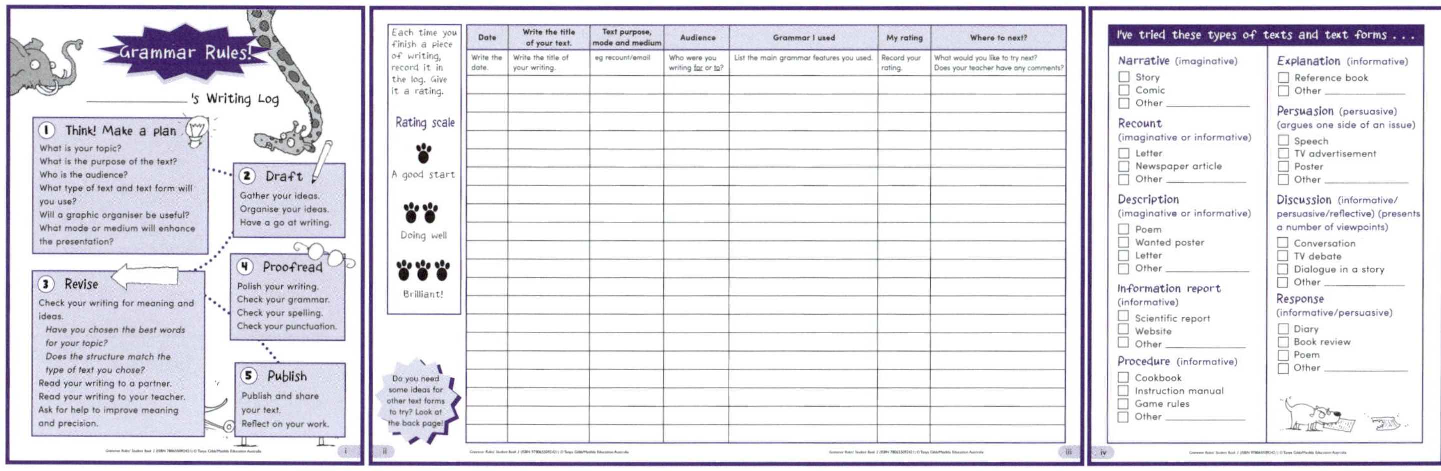

Sequenced activities
Activities focus on reading comprehension, text features and structures, vocabulary or punctuation

Rule!
Introduces students to a new concept

Text sample
Provides a context for learning about language

Unit tag
States the main grammar focus

Type of text
Highlights the type of text and purpose of the sample text

Try it yourself!
Gives students opportunities to apply their knowledge and skills to create their own texts. Students can engage in planning, drafting and editing their texts and use different modes and media to enhance presentation of their texts.

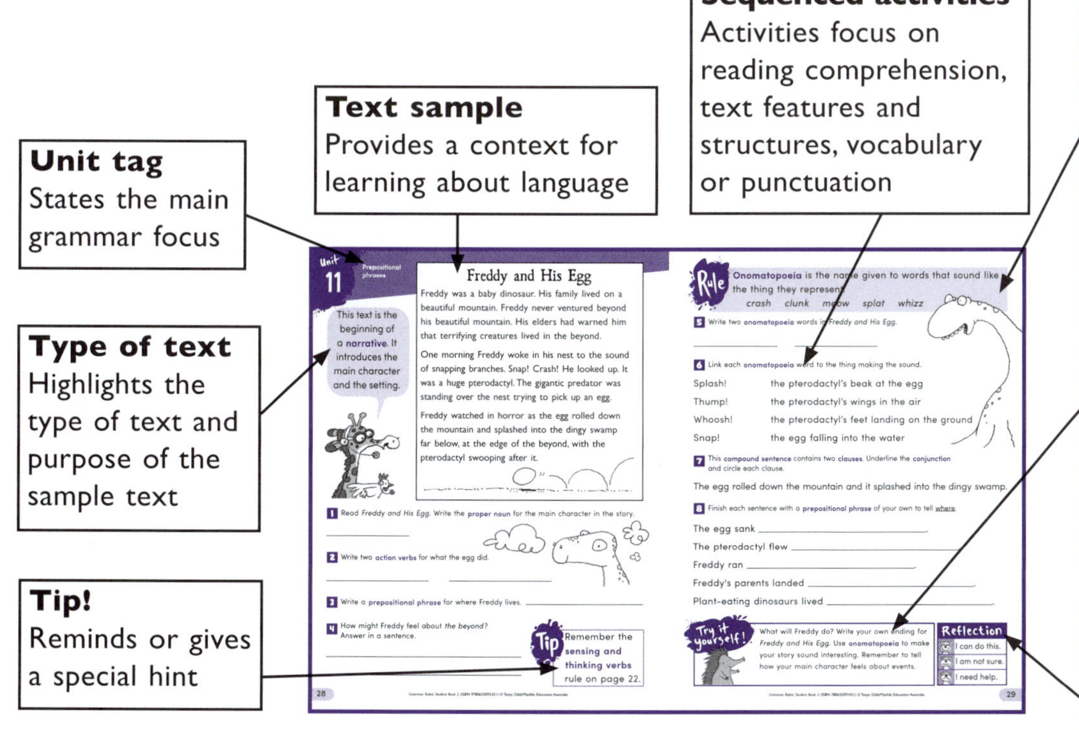

Tip!
Reminds or gives a special hint

Reflection
Encourages students to assess their progress through each activity

Grammar Rules! Teacher Resource Book 1–2

Full teacher support for *Student Book 2* is provided by *Grammar Rules! Teacher Resource Book 1–2*.

Here you will find valuable background information about teaching English along with practical resources, such as:

- strategies for teaching text structures and features
- literacy games and activities
- assessment strategies
- teaching tips for every unit in *Student Book 2*
- answers for every unit in *Student Book 2*.

Scope and Sequence

This scope and sequence chart is based on the requirements of the NSW English K–2 Syllabus.

Unit	Unit name Type of text	Purpose of text	Clauses, sentences, conjunctions	Nouns, noun groups, pronouns, adjectives	Verbs	Adverbs and prepositional phrases (time and place), time connectives	Elements of language
1	**Life Cycle of a Bird** Diagram	to inform		nouns	action verbs		
2	**Bee** Diagram	to inform	clauses, simple sentences		relating verbs		
3	**Move It!** Poem	to entertain	sentences, commas		action verbs		commas in a series
4	**Sloths** Report	to inform	clauses, simple sentences	nouns	verbs		
5	**Flies** Conversation	to inform and share opinions	exclamations, quoted speech		saying verbs		dialogue
6	REVISION						
7	**Children's Python** Recount	to inform		adjectives			
8	**The Best Pet** Argument	to persuade		adjectives	sensing and thinking verbs		antonyms, opinions and reasons
9	**Dear Gran and Pa** Recount	to inform	coordinating conjunctions			time connectives	
10	**Where's My Mum?** Narrative	to entertain	conjunctions, sentences			prepositions, prepositional phrases	
11	**Freddy and His Egg** Narrative	to entertain				prepositional phrases	onomatopoeia, story characters
12	REVISION						
13	**How To Help Insects** Instructions	to inform/ instruct	commands	personal pronouns			
14	**Lost Dog** Map	to inform	directions, commands		action verbs		compound words
15	**A Loony Cat** Description	to inform		personal pronouns			synonyms
16	**How** Poem	to entertain		singular and plural nouns		adverbs	
17	**Hypnotic** Response	to inform		noun groups, adjectives			opinions and reasons
18	REVISION						

Grammar Rules! Student Book 2 (ISBN 9780655092421) © Tanya Gibb/Matilda Education Australia

Unit	Unit name Type of text	Purpose of text	Clauses, sentences, conjunctions	Nouns, noun groups, pronouns, adjectives	Verbs	Adverbs and prepositional phrases (time and place), time connectives	Elements of language
19	**Giant Pandas** Response	to inform		noun groups			opinions and reasons
20	**Wildlife Carer** Interview	to inform	questions and statements				fact and opinion
21	**How The Land Was Formed** Retelling	to inform		articles, noun groups			
22	**Along Came a Spider** Narrative	to entertain	exclamations, quoted speech				
23	**Llamas for Sale** Advertisement	to persuade	exclamations, questions				emotive words
24	REVISION						
25	**Zoos** Discussion	to persuade	reported speech				paragraphs, apostrophes for possession
26	**How do Penguins Chicks Eat?** Explanation	to inform	questions	noun groups		prepositional phrases	
27	**Reptile Encounter** Recount	to inform	dependent and main clauses	conjunctions			contractions
28	**"Talk to the Animals" Potion** Recipe	to entertain			subject–verb agreement		alliteration, rhyme
29	**Ringtail Possums** Report	to inform			subject–verb agreement	prepositional phrases	topic sentences
30	REVISION						
31	**Corroboree Frogs** Report	to inform	clauses, conjunctions				
32	**The Chimp and the Crocodile** Narrative	to entertain			tense		
33	**How to Look After a Tarantula** Instructions	to inform	sentences		subject–verb agreement		
34	**How Sea Animals Breathe** Explanation	to inform	subordinating conjunctions, clauses, the subject of a clause				
35	REVISION						

Unit 1

Nouns, action verbs

Life Cycle of a Bird

The purpose of the diagram is to present information using drawings, labels and arrows.

1 Copy the simple sentences into the correct boxes on the diagram. These labels explain the life cycle of a bird.

The parent bird feeds the baby bird.
A chick grows inside the egg.
The mother bird lays an egg.
The young bird flies out of the nest.
The chick cracks out of the egg.
The parent birds build a nest.

Grammar Rules! Student Book 2 (ISBN 9780655092421)

Rule

Common nouns are everyday naming words.

family beaches birds chairs

Proper nouns name specific people, places, animals and things. They start with an **upper-case letter**.

Emily Newcastle Wollemi Pine Glossy Black-Cockatoo

2 Write four **common nouns** used in *Life Cycle of a Bird*.

____

Verbs are words or word groups that tell what is happening in a clause. **Action verbs** tell the actions.

is eating wriggles dangled swooped

3 Circle the **action verb** in each set of words.

branch nest feathers chew

home swoop magpie noisy

hatchling parent gulp leaf

flutter beautiful beak pretty

4 Choose an **action verb** from the box to complete each sentence.

dangled	opened	laid	grow	built

The mother bird ____________ three eggs.

The parents ____________ their nest on a high branch.

Chicks ____________ feathers.

The parent ____________ a worm for the chick.

The chick's mouth ____________.

Choose an animal. It might be one that lays eggs, such as a crocodile, a platypus or a dinosaur. Find out about the animal's life cycle. Draw a diagram with labels to explain each stage in the life cycle.

Reflection

 I can do this.

 I am not sure.

 I need help.

This **diagram** is informative. It has labels to show the parts of a bee.

Bee

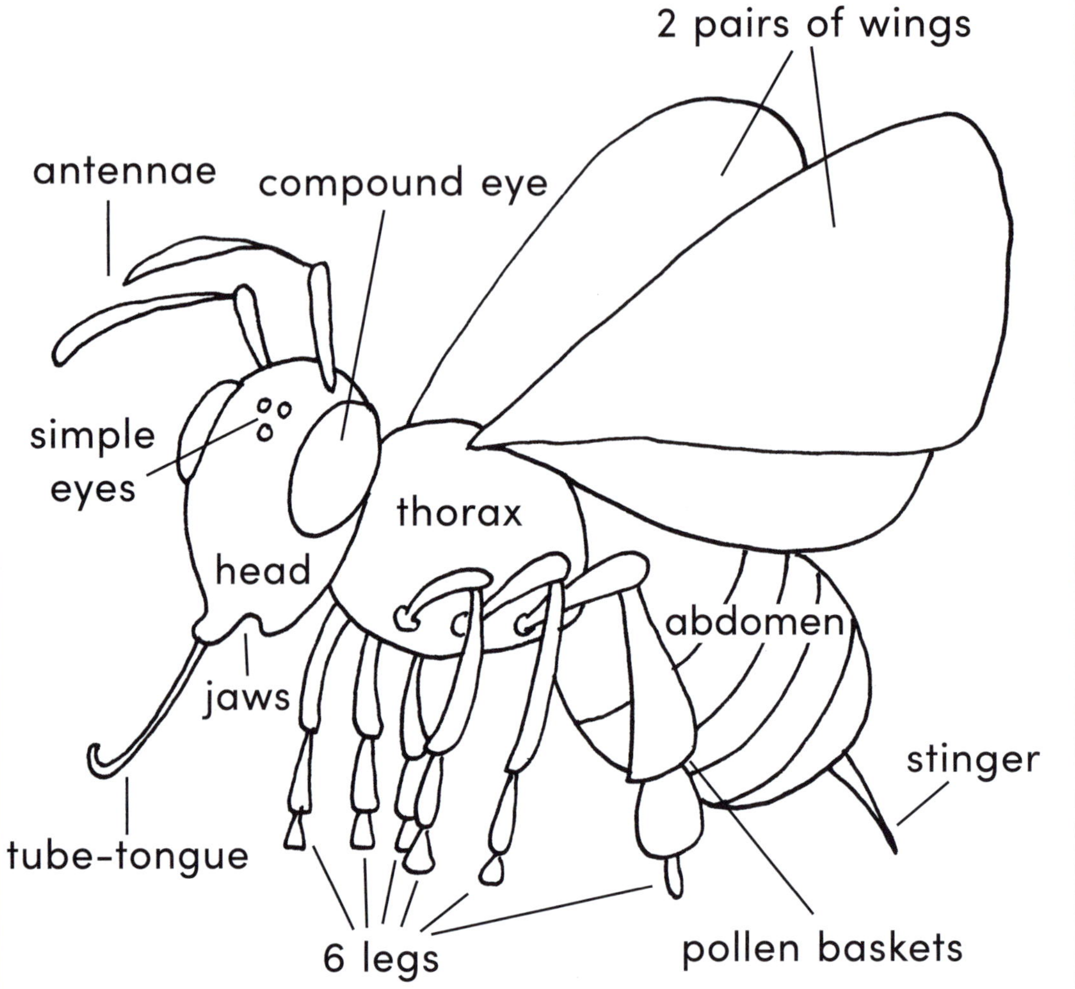

2 pairs of wings

antennae

compound eye

simple eyes

head

thorax

abdomen

jaws

stinger

tube-tongue

6 legs

pollen baskets

1 Look at the *Bee* diagram. Use a **common noun** to complete each sentence.

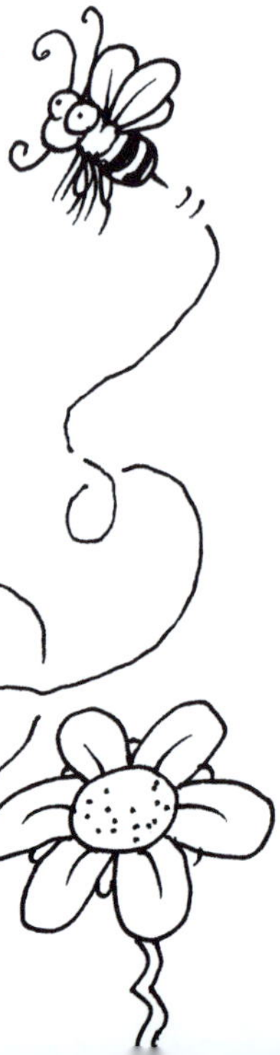

wings	legs	baskets	head	stinger

A bee's legs and ____________ are attached to its thorax.

Pollen ____________ are on the back legs.

The ____________ is on the end of the abdomen.

The antennae are on the bee's ____________.

Bees have six ____________.

Relating verbs show what things <u>are</u> or what things <u>have</u>. You cannot see any action taking place.

is am are was were has have had

2 Use a **relating verb** from the box to complete each sentence.

are
have
am
has
was

Bees _________ insects.

Bees _________ a stinger.

A bee _________ black stripes on an orange body.

I _________ fond of honey.

Eric _________ careful not to step on the bee.

A **sentence** is a complete message. A sentence can be made up of one or more **clauses**. Every clause must have a **verb**. A simple sentence is one clause.

3 Write the words in the correct order to form **simple sentences**. Remember that a sentence begins with an **upper-case letter** and ends with a full stop, question mark or exclamation mark.

in their hives honey make bees

____

bees only female stingers have

____

good for sucking tube-tongues are nectar

____

Make up a crazy insect. Create a **diagram**. Label the body parts. Now write three sentences to describe it. Use **relating verbs**.

Action verbs, sentences, commas

This poem lists the ways animals move. Its stanzas and sentences follow a regular pattern.

Move It!

Frogs leap,
hop, jump, swim.

Crocodiles run,
crawl, dive, roll.

Owls swoop,
fly, soar, glide.

Snakes slither,
slide, curl, sleep.

1 What is the poem about?

____

____

Rule

Commas are used to separate parts of a sentence or words in a series.

Remember to buy apples, bananas, watermelon and pineapple.

2 Rewrite the sentences using punctuation markers to match the poem.

fleas crawl jump cling irritate

____

dolphins swim glide dive jump

____

3 Write four **common nouns** for other animals that swim.

__________ __________ __________ __________

4 Write four **common nouns** for other animals that jump.

__________ __________ __________ __________

5 Underline the **action verbs** in *Move It!*

Grammar Rules! Student Book 2 (ISBN 9780655092421) © Tanya Gibb/Matilda Education Australia

6 Draw a line to match a **common noun** with an **action verb**.

A horse	hovers.
A camel	gallops.
A monkey	prowls.
A shark	swings.
A fly	lopes.

7 Rewrite the sentence by adding the punctuation markers.

allegra saw many cockatoos magpies butterflies and lizards on her walk

____

____

8 Write an **action verb** to tell how each animal moves.

A worm ______________________.
A lion ______________________.
An elephant ______________________.
A zebra ______________________.
A flea ______________________.
A mouse ______________________.

9 Circle the three **action verbs** that describe your best moves.

running dancing jumping creeping skating hiding
tickling hopping throwing

10 Circle the **action verbs** for what the wombat is doing.

claws digging burrowing swimming hole dirt mound tunnelling

Try it yourself!

Write a poem of your own using **action verbs**.
Read your poem to a group or the class.

Reflection

I can do this.
I am not sure.
I need help.

Unit 4

Simple sentences, clauses, verbs, nouns

This is an informative text. It is an **information report** about sloths.

Sloths

Sloths are mammals. They live in South America. Sloths have mostly brown fur. Sloths mainly eat leaves but sometimes they eat insects and lizards. Sloths are eaten by jaguars. Sloths sleep for at least fifteen hours every day. They spend a lot of time lying around in trees where they are hidden from view. When they are on the ground they walk very, very slowly. Sloths are probably the slowest animals on earth.

By Tsehay

1 Read *Sloths*. Write the **proper noun** for the place where sloths live.

____

2 Find a sentence in *Sloths* that includes a **relating verb**. Copy it onto the line.

____

3 Underline three **action verbs** in *Sloths* for actions sloths do.

The **subject** of a **clause** is the "who" or "what" that is doing the action.

Sloths sleep a lot. (Sloths are doing the sleeping.)

4 Use an **action verb** from the box to complete each **clause**. Circle the subject of each clause.

sleep	eat	walk	hide	climb

Sloths __________ leaves.

Sloths __________ trees.

Sloths __________ slowly.

Sloths __________ from jaguars.

Sloths __________ most of the day.

Grammar Rules! Student Book 2 (ISBN 9780655092421) © Tanya Gibb/Matilda Education Australia

5 Use a **common noun** from the box to complete each **simple sentence** with its subject.

Giraffes	Elephants	Koalas	Jaguars	Sloths

_______________ eat sloths.

_______________ reach into tall trees.

_______________ swing their trunks.

_______________ move slowly.

_______________ eat gum leaves.

6 Circle the **relating verbs** in these **sentences**.

Sloths are tree-dwelling mammals. They have mostly brown fur and are slow-moving, especially when they are on the ground.

7 Write the words in the correct order to form **simple sentences**. Use an **upper-case letter** to start each sentence. Use a full stop at the end.

on the branch the sloth sleeps

____

hugs a mother sloth its baby

____

the jaguar dinner hunts for

____

Choose an animal. Write an **information report** about the animal. Tell where it lives, what it looks like, what eats it and how it moves.

Unit 5

Saying verbs, exclamations, quoted speech

This text is a conversation. Each speaker's purpose is to share an opinion.

Flies

"Flies have disgusting habits," announced Jessica.

"I agree!" said Bob. "They eat anything, even animal droppings."

"Yes," replied Jessica. "They stand anywhere they like, including on your food. They have hairs on their legs, which pick up germs and bits of other disgusting things."

"Yes, gross. Flies also vomit all the time and they vomit onto your food when they land on it. They are disgusting!" exclaimed Bob.

Rule **Saying verbs** are verbs that show you something is being said.

called *yelled* *whispered*

1 Read *Flies*. Underline the four **saying verbs** in *Flies*.

2 Circle the correct answer.

Jessica and Bob agree/disagree about flies.

3 Write two **proper nouns** used in *Flies*. ____________________ ____________________

Rule An **exclamation** is a sentence that shows strong emotion, or gives a warning or command. An **exclamation** ends in an exclamation mark. *Stop!* *I love it!*

4 Write Bob's exclamation in *Flies* on the line. ____

Grammar Rules! Student Book 2 (ISBN 9780655092421) © Tanya Gibb/Matilda Education Australia

Quoted speech is the actual speech someone says.
It is written inside **quotation marks**.

"Shoo fly!" shouted Meena.

5 In *Flies*, circle what Bob actually says. Use a different colour to circle what Jessica says. Work with a partner. Read out loud what Bob and Jessica say.

6 Add **quotation marks** where they belong.

I don't like flies said Hasan.

Me neither replied Julie.

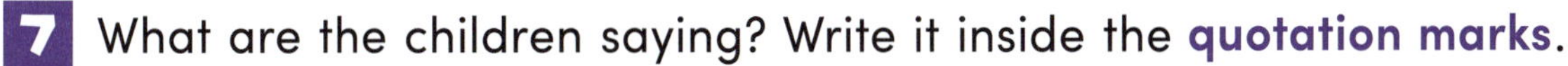

7 What are the children saying? Write it inside the **quotation marks**.

"________________________________," gulped Bob.

"________________________," yelled Jessica.

8 Write two **exclamations** you might make if a fly landed on your food.

Write a **conversation** between two people. Write their **quoted speech** inside **quotation marks**. Use **saying verbs** to show how something is being said.

Reflection

- I can do this.
- I am not sure.
- I need help.

Unit 6 Revision

1 Write the labels on the diagram. Put them in the correct order to explain the life cycle.

The larva then goes into its pupa stage.

An egg is laid.

The egg hatches into a larva.

The adult emerges.

The larva grows.

Life Cycle of a Beetle

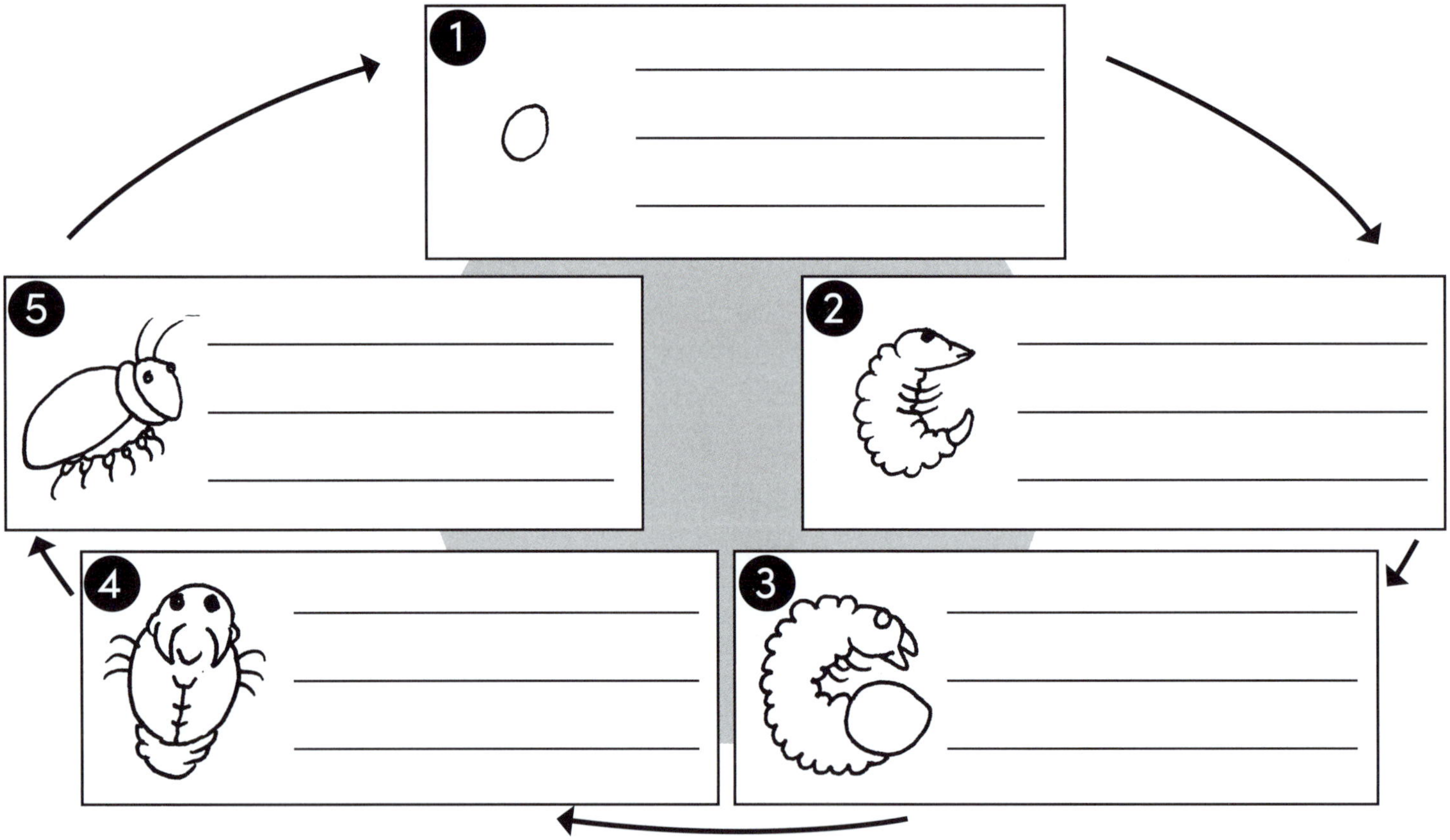

1 ______

2 ______

3 ______

4 ______

5 ______

2 Write four **common nouns** from the Life Cycle of a Beetle.

______

3 Circle the **verb** in each sentence. Underline the **proper nouns**.

Louie's hamster ran away.

The mouse in Mr Augustine's pet shop had babies.

Possums live in the roof of Cate's house.

"Beetles have six legs," stated Ms Holliday.

Grammar Rules! Student Book 2 (ISBN 9780655092421)

4 Rewrite each sentence. Use **upper-case letters**, **full stops** and **quotation marks**.

next tuesday I am going on an excursion to the zoo, said dean

____

mona patted a koala yelled sebastian

____

5 Write an **action verb** from the box in each **simple sentence**.

picked	buzzed	kicked	shared	climbed

A goat ________________ the mountain.

Flies ________________ around the cake.

Moana ________________ her banana.

Leila ________________ the ball.

Ollie ________________ strawberries.

6 Write the words in the correct order to form **sentences**. Use correct punctuation.

pond the croak in frogs

____

sloths jaguars eat

____

like climb to goats mountains

____

7 Write a **relating verb** on each line.

Bees __________ insects. They __________ six legs and two antennae.

Those broken glasses __________ Zoe's. Luckily, she __________ a spare pair.

The writer's purpose is to recount an experience and give an opinion about it.

Children's Python

My younger sister and I went to a talk at the zoo. It was interesting. The zookeeper showed us a Children's python. The species was named in 1842 after a man at a museum in England whose name was John George Children.

The python was beautiful. She was brown with darker brown splotches. Her skin felt smooth and was as soft as silk. When she was warm from being handled she became more active. Children's pythons can bite but she was very gentle and placid.

I enjoyed learning about the Children's python.

By Lottie

1 Read *Children's Python*. Underline four **common nouns**.

2 What is the writer's opinion about the talk at the zoo? Answer in a **sentence**.

---

3 What is the writer's opinion about the Children's python? Answer in a **sentence**.

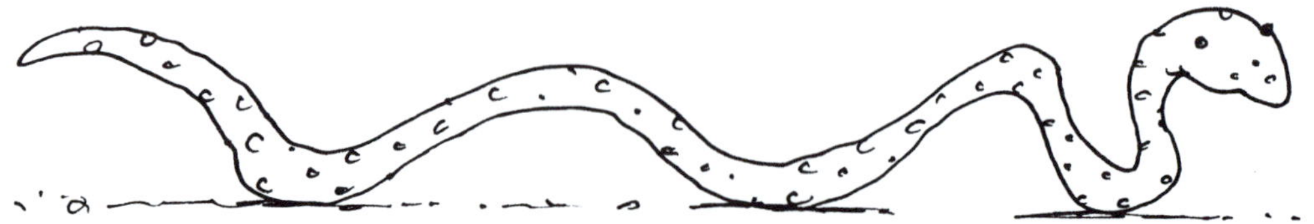

Grammar Rules! Student Book 2 (ISBN 9780655092421) © Tanya Gibb/Matilda Education Australia

Adjectives build descriptions of **nouns**. Adjectives help the writer share an opinion and help readers form opinions.

cute kitten *timid dog* *sad monkey*

4 Find **adjectives** in *Children's Python* to describe these **common nouns**.

____________ sister ____________ splotches ____________ skin

____________ skin ____________ snake ____________ snake

5 Find three **adjectives** in *Children's Python* that tell you the writer has a good opinion of the snake.

____________ ____________ ____________

6 Describe the animals. Write an **adjective** from the box on each line.

heavy	tiny	tall	toothy	sleepy

__________ __________ __________ __________ __________

7 Finish the **sentence**.

The python's skin was as ____________ as ____________.

8 Circle the **adjectives** that might describe a dog you should NOT pat.

active greedy placid brown scary ferocious quiet soft

Try it yourself!

Write about an experience you have had. It could be about somewhere you have been or something you have done. Describe it and give your opinion about it.

Reflection

- I can do this.
- I am not sure.
- I need help.

The writer's purpose is to present an opinion and persuade others to accept that opinion.

The Best Pet

I think mice are the best pets for these reasons:

They are fun to watch when they run on their exercise wheel and play with their toys.

They are really small so they are good pets if you live in a unit.

They are simple to care for – just keep their home clean.

Their food costs very little.

Those are the reasons why I think mice are the best pets. If you want a pet, I recommend mice but get two so they keep each other company.

By Kai

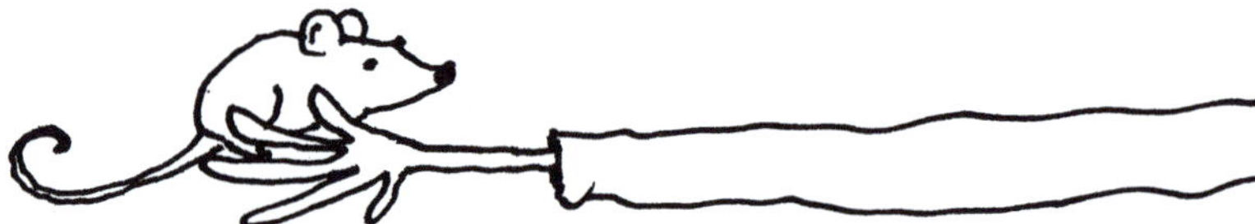

1 Read *The Best Pet*. Underline five **common nouns**.

2 What does Kai want people to believe? Write a **sentence** to answer.

____

3 The writer uses the relating verb "are" in *The Best Pet*. Circle it.

How many times is it used? ☐

Sensing and thinking verbs are words for activities you cannot see taking place (*feel, see, think, hope, wonder, decided, heard*). *The mouse saw the carrot. The egg smelled off. Kai feels sad.*

4 Complete each sentence with a **verb** from the box.

thinks feel want hope

I ____________ my pet mouse has babies.

I ____________ two mice.

Dad ____________ mice are fun to watch.

I ____________ very happy today.

5 Write two **sensing and thinking verbs** used in *The Best Pet*.

____________________ ____________________

6 Circle the **sensing and thinking verbs**.

worry agree wonder skip love jump

need concentrate like dislike cook understand

7 Write a **sentence** telling whether you agree or disagree with the writer of *The Best Pet* and why. Use **sensing and thinking verbs**.

____

8 Write a **sentence** that tells how you would feel about minding someone's pet mice for a few days.

____

Antonyms are words that mean opposite things.

hot → cold *reasonable → unreasonable*

9 Draw lines to link pairs of **antonyms**.

tall	smooth
thin	short
rough	quiet
loud	thick

10 Write an **antonym** for each **sensing or thinking verb**.

dishonest ________________

disagree ________________

disbelieve ________________

dislike ________________

Write a persuasive text about the animal you think is the best pet. Begin with a statement that gives your opinion. Then give your reasons. End with a summing up statement.

Unit 9 Conjunctions, time connectives

Sara
Re: Pet shop visit
To: Gran and Pa

Dear Gran and Pa,

I asked Mum for a puppy but dogs make Dad sneeze so we decided to buy goldfish.

Yesterday we went to the pet shop. First we had to buy a fish tank and gravel. Then we chose a bridge and some plants. After that I got to choose two fish. I picked a black one and a gold one. I've named them Midnight and Sundance.

You'd like them.

Love from Sara

This email is informative. It **recounts** events that have happened.

1 Read *Dear Gran and Pa*. Underline six **proper nouns**.

2 Write the **saying verb** used in *Dear Gran and Pa*.

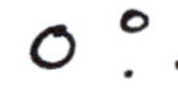

____

Rule

Coordinating **conjunctions** (*and, but, or, so*) are used to connect independent **clauses** in compound sentences.

I love oranges/and I love bananas.

I love oranges/but apples are my favourite fruit.

3 The first sentence in *Dear Gran and Pa* has two **conjunctions**. Circle them.

4 Write a sentence to show what Sara might say to her parents about the goldfish. Use **quotation marks**. Use a **saying verb**.

Tip Remember the **quoted speech** rule on page 17.

____

____

Rule **Time connectives** can help to sequence events in time.

first *next* *after* *then*

5 Reread *Dear Gran And Pa*. What did Sara do *first* at the pet shop?

____

Then what did she do? ______________________________

After that, what did she do? ______________________________

6 Use a **conjunction** from the box to join the **clauses** in each sentence. You can use any conjunction more than once.

and
but
or
so

Sara wanted a pet _______ she promised to look after it.

We could get a dog _______ Dad is allergic to dogs.

We'll buy a big tank _______ the fish will have lots of room.

We bought two fish _______ we bought fish food.

We can get a bridge _______ we can get a tunnel _______ we can't afford a bridge and a tunnel.

Sara now has goldfish _______ she can stop asking for a dog.

7 Write numbers 1 to 4 in the boxes to sequence the events in time.

☐ Finally I added the goldfish.

☐ After that, I filled the tank with water.

☐ First I cleaned the tank.

☐ Then I added gravel and plants.

Try it yourself!

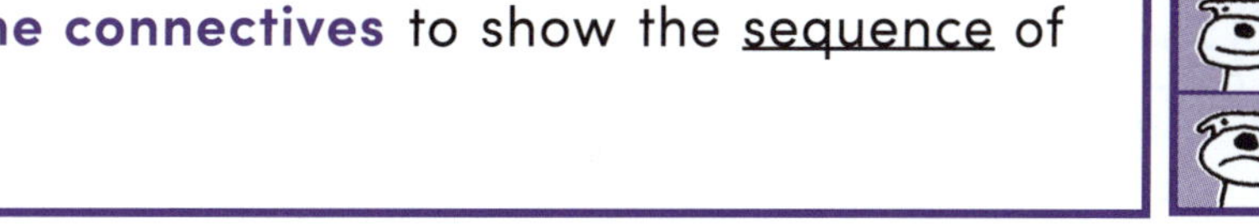

Write an email to a friend or family member. **Recount** something that you have done recently. Use **time connectives** to show the sequence of events.

Reflection

- I can do this.
- I am not sure.
- I need help.

Unit 10

Prepositions, prepositional phrases

Where's My Mum?

The duckling woke from a nap and could not see his mother. He asked all the animals on the farm,

"Have you seen my mother?"

He asked:

the cow under the tree,

the horse in the barn,

the cat on the branch,

the pig beside the trough,

the dog behind the gate,

the goose on the wood pile,

the chicken on the roof,

and the turtle near the tractor,

who said, "There she is."

1 Read *Where's My Mum?* Circle the **common nouns** for animals on the farm.

2 Mark the duckling's route around the farm. Use arrows. → → →

Grammar Rules! Student Book 2 (ISBN 9780655092421) © Tanya Gibb/Matilda Education Australia

A **prepositional phrase** is a unit of meaning that begins with a **preposition** (*in, on, beside, above, under*).
A prepositional phrase can tell where or when or how.

on a giant rock *under the waterfall* *with its beak*

3 Circle the **prepositional phrases** in *Where's My Mum?*

4 Add a **preposition** from the box to each sentence. Use the illustration in question 2 for clues.

around toward through onto beside

A turtle plodded ____________ the tractor.

The pig waited ____________ its trough.

The dog peered ____________ the railings.

The chicken fluttered ____________ the roof.

The duckling walked ____________ the farm.

5 Use a **conjunction** to join the **simple sentences**. Write each new sentence.

The duckling looked for his mother. He found her in the pond.

____

The tractor was not working. The farmer fixed it.

____

6 Use a **preposition** from the box to complete each sentence.

over among between

The goslings hid ____________ the reeds.

We tied our hammock ____________ two trees.

The horse jumped ____________ the fence.

Draw a map to illustrate a **narrative** that you have written. Include places on the map that your characters visit. Mark their route.

Reflection

- I can do this.
- I am not sure.
- I need help.

This text is the beginning of a **narrative**. It introduces the main character and the setting.

Freddy and His Egg

Freddy was a baby dinosaur. His family lived on a beautiful mountain. Freddy never ventured beyond his beautiful mountain. His elders had warned him that terrifying creatures lived in the beyond.

One morning Freddy woke in his nest to the sound of snapping branches. Snap! Crash! He looked up. It was a huge pterodactyl. The gigantic predator was standing over the nest trying to pick up an egg.

Freddy watched in horror as the egg rolled down the mountain and splashed into the dingy swamp far below, at the edge of the beyond, with the pterodactyl swooping after it.

1 Read *Freddy and His Egg*. Write the **proper noun** for the main character in the story.

____

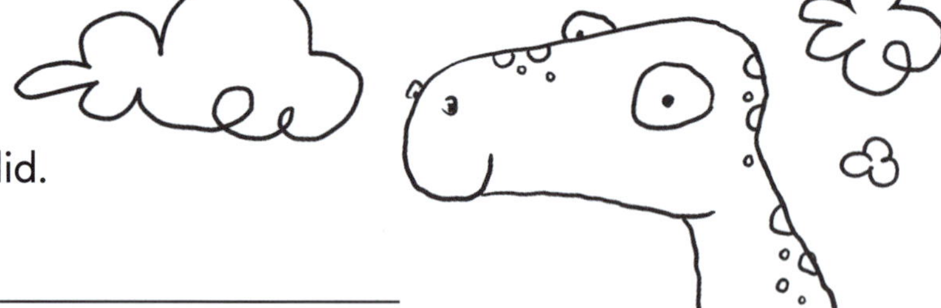

2 Write two **action verbs** for what the egg did.

______________________ ______________________

3 Write a **prepositional phrase** for where Freddy lives. ______________________

4 How might Freddy feel about *the beyond*? Answer in a sentence.

____

____

Remember the **sensing and thinking verbs** rule on page 22.

Grammar Rules! Student Book 2 (ISBN 9780655092421) © Tanya Gibb/Matilda Education Australia

Onomatopoeia is the name given to words that sound like the thing they represent.

crash *clunk* *meow* *splat* *whizz*

5 Write two **onomatopoeia** words in *Freddy and His Egg.*

______________________ ______________________

6 Link each **onomatopoeia** word to the thing making the sound.

Splash!	the pterodactyl's beak at the egg
Thump!	the pterodactyl's wings in the air
Whoosh!	the pterodactyl's feet landing on the ground
Snap!	the egg falling into the water

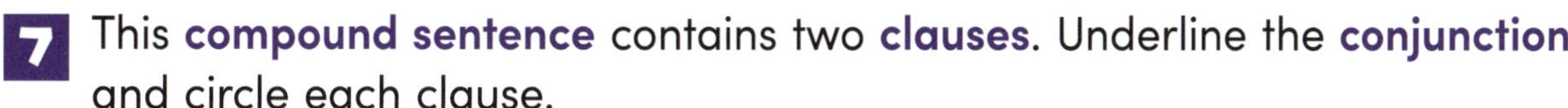

7 This **compound sentence** contains two **clauses**. Underline the **conjunction** and circle each clause.

The egg rolled down the mountain and it splashed into the dingy swamp.

8 Finish each sentence with a **prepositional phrase** of your own to tell <u>where</u>.

The egg sank ______________________________________.

The pterodactyl flew ______________________________________.

Freddy ran ______________________________________.

Freddy's parents landed ______________________________________.

Plant-eating dinosaurs lived ______________________________________.

What will Freddy do? Write your own ending for *Freddy and His Egg*. Use **onomatopoeia** to make your story sound interesting. Remember to tell how your main character feels about events.

Unit 12 Revision

1 Write a **prepositional phrase** on the lines below each animal to tell where it lives or hides.

 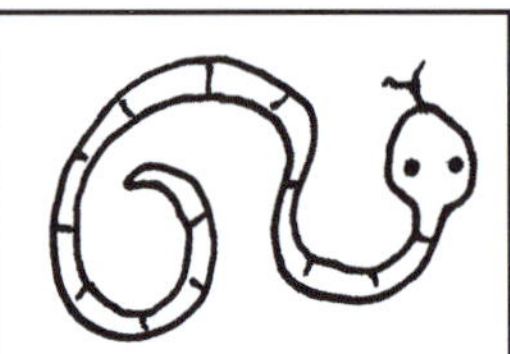   

2 Write a sentence for each **sensing or thinking verb** in the box.

thinks	feel	want	saw	imagine

3 Write an **antonym** for each word.

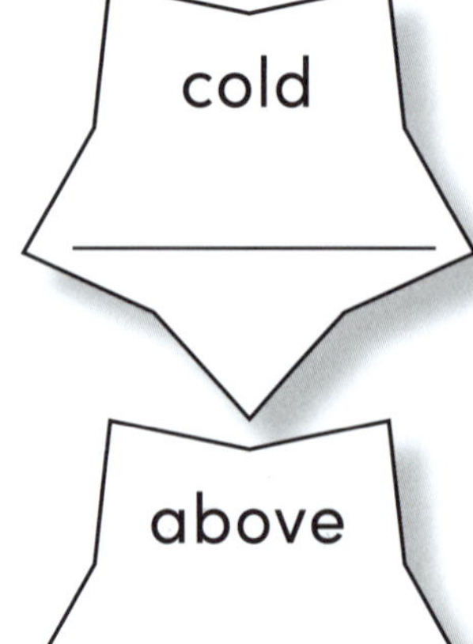

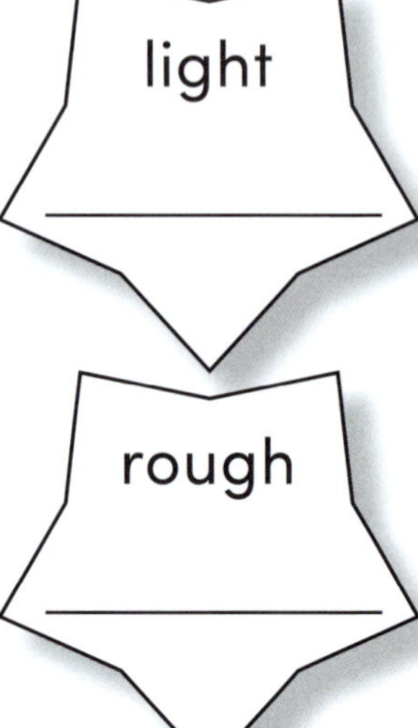

Grammar Rules! Student Book 2 (ISBN 9780655092421) © Tanya Gibb/Matilda Education Australia

4 Use a **conjunction** from the box to join the clauses in each sentence.

or	but	and

I like vanilla ice cream __________ I eat ice cream every Sunday.

We can go to the movies __________ we can watch a movie on TV.

I could do better at cricket __________ I don't enjoy cricket practice.

5 Use the **time connectives** in the box to show the correct sequence of events.

Then First Finally After

__________ I set up the tank.

__________ I let the tarantula settle into the tank.

__________ that I put in some crickets.

__________ the tarantula ate the crickets.

6 Write a sentence for each **relating verb** in the box.

is am are have had

____

____

____

____

____

7 Add an interesting **adjective** of your own to describe each **noun**.

the __________ dragon

two __________ black puppies

my __________ shoes

Sofia's __________ uncle

a __________ T-rex

a __________ bunch of grapes

a __________ holiday

an __________ story

a __________ bowl of freshly cooked noodles

The purpose of these **instructions** is to tell readers how to help insects.

How to Help Insects

We need insects to pollinate our plants and do other jobs for us. Insects need safe places to rest and to lay their eggs. You can help insects.

1. Avoid using pesticides.
2. Place small shallow plates of water with rocks in them in your garden so insects can land and have a drink.
3. Plant flowers, especially native flowers.
4. Leave a small corner of your garden in a natural state with bark and bare soil for ground-dwelling insects.

1 Why should you place a shallow plate of water in the garden?

____

2 Why should you avoid using pesticides?

____

3 Why should you leave bark on the ground?

____

4 Circle the **verb** that begins each instruction in *How to Help Insects.*

Rule

Commands are orders. They often begin with a **verb.**

Don't walk on the grass. *Do your homework.*

Instructions and directions are often written as commands. They tell what to do to achieve a goal.

5 Use an **action verb** from the box to begin each command.

Clean Feed Add Walk Pick

__________ the cat.

__________ the dog.

__________ the fish tank.

__________ up the dog's droppings.

__________ a bee hotel to the garden.

6 Write a **command** that a family member gives you. Use quoted speech with **quotation marks**.

____

Rule

A **personal pronoun** is a word that is used in place of a **noun**.

me I we us you he him she her it they them

I need that book. Will you pass it to me, please?

7 Underline three **personal pronouns** in *How to Help Insects*.

8 Use a **personal pronoun** from the box to replace the noun in brackets in each sentence. If the pronoun begins a sentence use an **upper-case letter** to start.

he them they him

(Harry) ________ is making a bee hotel. Give the bamboo to ________ (Harry).

(Marika and Georgie) ________ are going to the park. Would you like to go to the park with ________ (Marika and Georgie)?

Try it yourself!

Write a set of **instructions** to tell a reader how to do something. Have a classmate read your instructions to check that they are clear and easy to follow.

Reflection

- I can do this.
- I am not sure.
- I need help.

This **map** is informative. It shows the location of things in the neighbourhood.

Lost Dog

Charlie's dog, Jet, has wandered away from home. Charlie has placed "LOST DOG" posters all over the neighbourhood. Help Charlie find Jet.

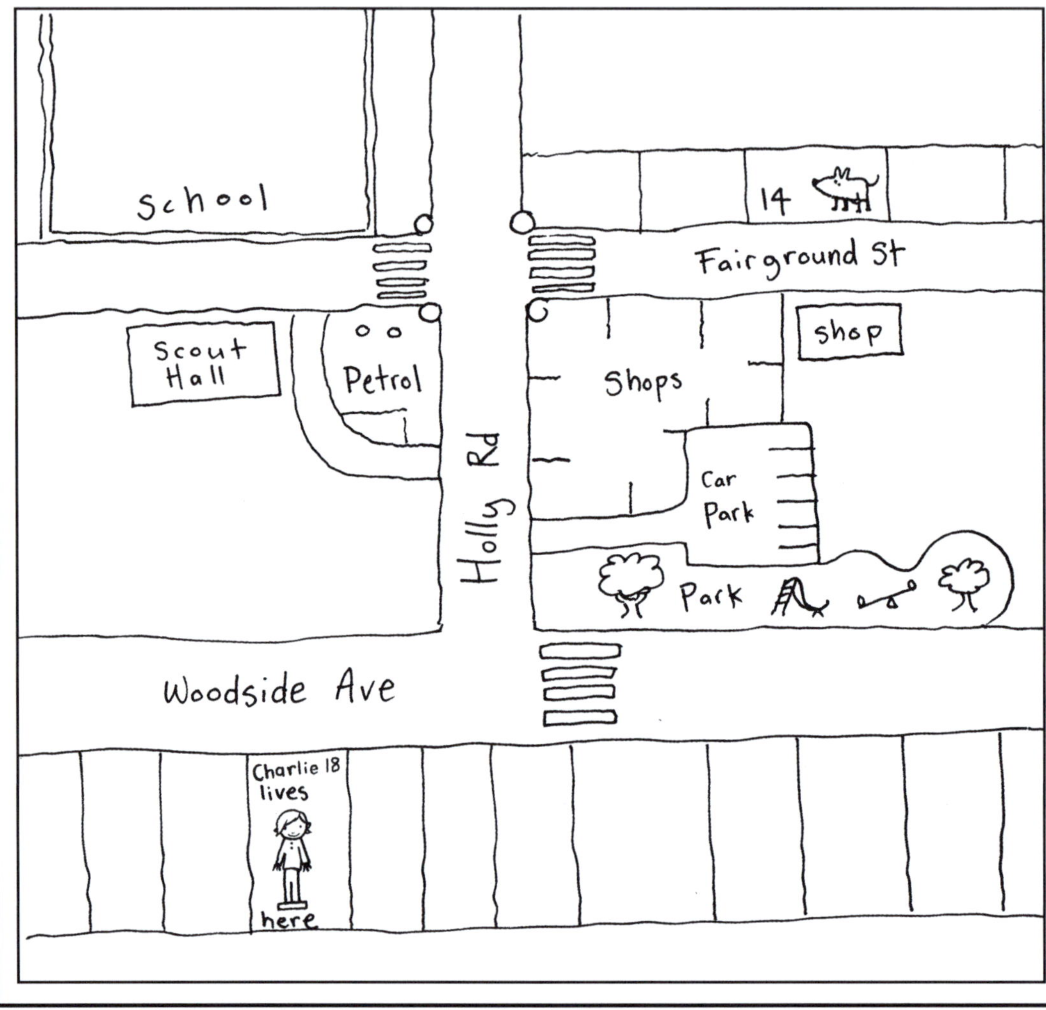

1 Look at the map. Look for Charlie. Look for Jet. Mark the route on the map with arrows and then write the directions below. Use **action verbs** to start each **command**.

____

____

____

____

2 List three places Charlie will pass on the way to Jet.

____

Grammar Rules! Student Book 2 (ISBN 9780655092421) © Tanya Gibb/Matilda Education Australia

Compound words are words that are formed by combining two other words.

Sunday blueberry classroom cardboard rainbow

3 Draw a line to match the parts of the **compound words**.

back	noon
play	yard
ship	day
after	ground
birth	paper
news	wreck

4 Write a **compound word** for each illustration.

+ = ______________

 + = ______________

+ = ______________

+  = ______________

+ = ______________

5 Circle the **action verbs** that you can do with a dog.

run mouth chase toes walk fetch teeth ears feet head tongue roll play feed tail tickle scratch pat nose wrestle lick leash

6 Write a **sentence** to describe a dog of your choice. Use **adjectives**.

____

____

7 What would Charlie have said to the person who found Jet? Use **quoted speech**.

____

____

Try it yourself!

Make a poster about Charlie's lost dog. Include **adjectives** to **describe** the dog. Write where it was last seen, its name, information about any reward and Charlie's contact phone number. Include a picture of the dog.

Reflection

 I can do this.

 I am not sure.

 I need help.

Unit 15

Personal pronouns, synonyms

The writer's purpose is to describe their cat's behaviour.

A Loony Cat

Catnip is a herb. You can grow it in the garden. When you break open a catnip leaf you release a chemical that a large number of cats really love.

I have a cat that goes berserk when she smells catnip. She leaps and runs and pounces on the catnip leaf. She rolls on it and over it. She scratches it and paws at it. She licks it and then chews it, but then she spits it out. Then she growls and purrs and meows at it until she is exhausted. Then she has a catnap. She is really very funny to watch.

I think she deserves an award for craziest cat.

1 Why is the title of the text *A Loony Cat*?

____

2 Write five **action verbs** for things the cat does.

__________ __________ __________ __________ __________

3 Write the two **compound words** used in *A Loony Cat*.

__________ __________

4 Write four **common nouns** used in *A Loony Cat*.

__________ __________ __________ __________

Grammar Rules! Student Book 2 (ISBN 9780655092421) © Tanya Gibb/Matilda Education Australia

5 In *A Loony Cat,* circle the words *catnip* and *catnip leaf.* Then circle *it.* *It* is a **personal pronoun** that is used in place of *catnip* and *catnip leaf.* Read *A Loony Cat* to yourself, using *the catnip leaf* instead of *it* when you read. What do you think about the **personal pronoun** *it* after your reading?

____

6 Which **personal pronoun** is used in place of the noun *cat*? ______________

How many times is this **pronoun** used in *A Loony Cat*? __________

7 Add a **personal pronoun** to each line.

Lata and Matt have a new male cat. _______ have called _______ Leo. _______ got _______ from the RSPCA. Leo was an adult when they got _______ but _______ was only tiny. Lata says Leo is very happy living with _______ . _______ love Leo.

Rule

A **synonym** is a word that has a similar meaning to another word.

8 Write words from *A Loony Cat* that are **synonyms** for the words below.

adore ______________

big ______________

crazy ______________

9 Use a dictionary. What does *berserk* mean?

____

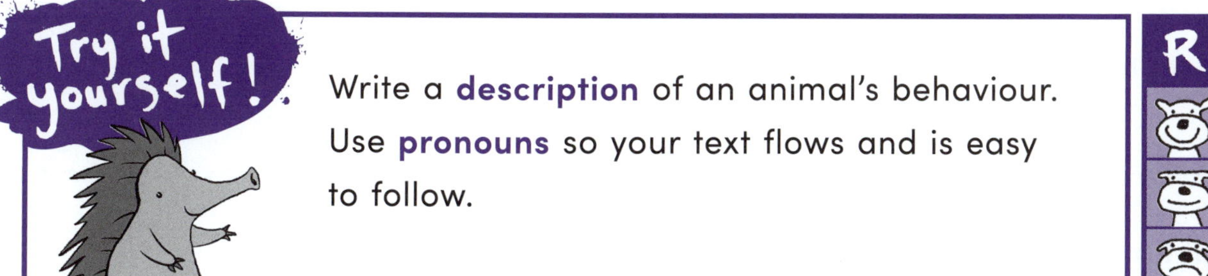

Write a **description** of an animal's behaviour. Use **pronouns** so your text flows and is easy to follow.

Reflection

I can do this.

I am not sure.

I need help.

Unit 16

Singular and plural nouns, adverbs

This poem uses **adverbs** to tell how the animals move or behave.

How

Cats creep quietly
on soft pads.
Zebras run swiftly
with powerful legs.
Woodpeckers knock loudly
on the trunks of trees.
Penguin chicks sit warmly
on parents' feet.
Bear teeth rot easily
from too many sweets.
I sleep happily
in my cosy bed.

1 Read *How*. Underline the **action verbs**.

Rule

A **noun** is **singular** for one thing. *toad*

A **noun** is **plural** for more than one thing. *toads*

A noun can be made **plural** by:

- adding *–s* or *–es* on the end *parent → parents*, *peach → peaches*
- changing *–y* to *i* to add *–es* *baby → babies*
- changing the spelling in another way *foot → feet*

Some nouns don't change at all from single to plural.

fish *sheep*

2 Write five **plural nouns** from *How* that end in *–s*.

____

3 Write a **plural noun** in *How* that does not end in *–s*. ______________

Adverbs modify verbs (*Cats creep quietly.*), **adjectives** (*Catnip is really special.*) and other **adverbs** (*Cats creep very quietly.*). Many adverbs end in *-ly*.

4 Circle six **adverbs** used in *How*.

5 Complete each extra **sentence** for the poem. Follow the same pattern as the poem.

Noun/pronoun	Verb	Adverb	Prepositional phrase
e.g. I	*sleep*	*happily*	*in my cosy bed.*
Dogs			
Dolphins			
Possums			
Snakes			

6 Use an **adverb** from the box to complete each sentence.

loudly madly widely menacingly

The elephant trumpeted ________________.

The tiger prowled ________________.

The wolf howled ________________.

The hippo yawned ________________.

7 Write a **plural** for each **singular noun**.

horse ____________ elephant ____________ salmon ____________

fox ____________ mouse ____________ ostrich ____________

Write a poem. Use **adverbs** ending in *-ly* to add meaning to the **verbs**. Your poem might describe actions of animals, your own actions or actions in sport.

Reflection

 I can do this.

 I am not sure.

 I need help.

Unit 17

Adjectives, noun groups

The writer's purpose is to give an **opinion** about a painting. The opinion is supported with **reasons.**

Hypnotic

My favourite painting is a painting of a leopard. It was painted by wildlife artist Alan Hunt. He always paints pictures of endangered animals. The painting is called *Hypnotic*. The beautiful leopard is lying along the branch of a tree. Two legs and the tail are dangling from the branch. The leopard looks relaxed and alert at the same time. It could pounce at any moment. The leopard is brown, cream and gold. These are also the colours of the bush.

I think the painting is very clever.

1 Write the **prepositional phrase** that tells where the leopard is lying.

____

2 Look up "hypnotic" in a dictionary. Why do you think the painting is called *Hypnotic*?

____

3 Find six **adjectives** in *Hypnotic* that describe what the leopard looks like.

__________ __________ __________

__________ __________ __________

4 What two **nouns** does the **pronoun** *It* refer to in *Hypnotic?*

____

5 What **noun** does the **personal pronoun** *He* replace? __________

Grammar Rules! Student Book 2 (ISBN 9780655092421) © Tanya Gibb/Matilda Education Australia

Grammar Rules!

_______________________ 's Writing Log

1 Think! Make a plan

What is your topic?
What is the purpose of the text?
Who is the audience?
What type of text and text form will you use?
Will a graphic organiser be useful?
What mode or medium will enhance the presentation?

2 Draft

Gather your ideas.
Organise your ideas.
Have a go at writing.

3 Revise

Check your writing for meaning and ideas.

Have you chosen the best words for your topic?
Does the structure match the type of text you chose?

Read your writing to a partner.
Read your writing to your teacher.
Ask for help to improve meaning and precision.

4 Proofread

Polish your writing.
Check your grammar.
Check your spelling.
Check your punctuation.

5 Publish

Publish and share your text.
Reflect on your work.

Each time you finish a piece of writing, record it in the log. Give it a rating.

Rating scale

A good start

Doing well

Brilliant!

Do you need some ideas for other text forms to try? Look at the back page!

Date	Write the title of your text.	Text purpose, mode and medium	Audience
Write the date.	Write the title of your writing.	eg recount/email	Who were you writing <u>for</u> or <u>to</u>?

Grammar Rules! Student Book 2 (ISBN 9780655092421) © Tanya Gibb/Matilda Education Australia

Grammar I used	My rating	Where to next?
List the main grammar features you used.	Record your rating.	What would you like to try next? Does your teacher have any comments?

I've tried these types of texts and text forms . . .

Narrative (imaginative)

- ☐ Story
- ☐ Comic
- ☐ Other ________________

Recount

(imaginative or informative)

- ☐ Letter
- ☐ Newspaper article
- ☐ Other ________________

Description

(imaginative or informative)

- ☐ Poem
- ☐ Wanted poster
- ☐ Letter
- ☐ Other ________________

Information report

(informative)

- ☐ Scientific report
- ☐ Website
- ☐ Other ________________

Procedure (informative)

- ☐ Cookbook
- ☐ Instruction manual
- ☐ Game rules
- ☐ Other ________________

Explanation (informative)

- ☐ Reference book
- ☐ Other ________________

Persuasion (persuasive)

(argues one side of an issue)

- ☐ Speech
- ☐ TV advertisement
- ☐ Poster
- ☐ Other ________________

Discussion (informative/ persuasive/reflective) (presents a number of viewpoints)

- ☐ Conversation
- ☐ TV debate
- ☐ Dialogue in a story
- ☐ Other ________________

Response

(informative/persuasive)

- ☐ Diary
- ☐ Book review
- ☐ Poem
- ☐ Other ________________

Rule

A **noun group** is a group of words that includes a **noun**. A noun group can begin with an **article** (*a, an, the*) and include **adjectives** that describe (*an amazing painting*) or tell quantity (*four magpies, some grapes*).

6 Write the correct **article** (*a, an, the, The*) on each line.

Zali saw ______ interesting artwork in ______ art gallery.

______ artwork was by Dr Treahna Hamm, ______ artist from ______ Wiradjuri and Yorta Yorta nations.

7 Circle the **noun groups**.

Al rescued a huntsman spider.

The television remote is broken.

We watched an entertaining show.

Jamal wrote a rhyming poem.

Year 2 went to the art gallery.

Ava enjoys Dreaming stories.

8 Underline the **adjectives** that tell quantity.

Bernie was first in line.

Frogs lay many eggs.

Three crocodiles swam past.

A few children are absent today.

9 Complete each sentence with **adjectives** from the box.

juicy grassy hungry sleek dirty oozy

The __________ dog rolled in the __________ mud.

The __________ horse galloped across the __________ paddock.

The __________ caterpillar ate the __________ leaf.

Try it yourself!

Write your **opinion** about an artwork you have seen or a book you have read. Say what you like or dislike about it. Use **adjectives**.

Reflection
I can do this.
I am not sure.
I need help.

Unit 18

Revision

1 Use an **action verb** from the box to begin each **command**.

Buy	Run	Check	Mix	Take

__________ the letterbox.

__________ to the bus stop.

__________ a loaf of bread.

__________ this to the principal.

__________ the paint carefully.

2 Draw lines to match the parts of the **compound words**.

day	top
tooth	fall
door	light
water	brush
desk	bell

3 Write a **personal pronoun** on each line.

Cockatiels are a kind of parrot. __________ are smaller than cockatoos. Like a cockatoo, a cockatiel has a crest on its head, which __________ uses for communication. Cockatiels are about 30 cm tall. __________ have bright orange circles on their cheeks.

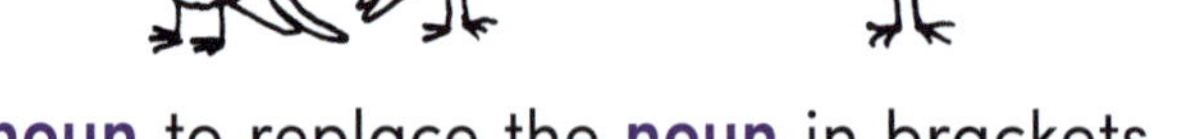

4 Use a **personal pronoun** to replace the **noun** in brackets.

He
She
It
They
them

(Mum) __________ is breeding frogs.

Give the worms to __________ (the fish).

(Tom) __________ loves Siamese fighting fish.

(The families) __________ are going to the school fete.

(The crocodile) __________ has sharp teeth.

5 Use an **adverb** from the box to complete each sentence.

slowly cheekily bravely

Fifi ____________ hissed at the dog.

The turtle ____________ crawled away.

The monkey danced ____________.

6 Write a word from the box on each line to create **synonym** pairs.

tasty	chilly	gigantic	simple	little	horrible

awful ____________ cold ____________ easy ____________

huge ____________ delicious ____________ small ____________

7 Write a **plural** for each **singular** noun.

rabbit ____________ monkey ____________ walrus ____________

emu ____________ platypus ____________ echidna ____________

8 Underline the **noun groups**.

A funnel-web spider is hiding in there.

Charlotte caught the basketball.

Javier enjoys crossword puzzles.

9 Add one word from each box to each sentence to create noun groups.
Use an **upper-case letter** if the adjective begins a sentence.

two	some	first	few

school	tomato	Siamese	football

Hossein ate ____________ ____________ sandwiches for lunch.

____________ dogs chased after the ____________ cat.

A ____________ fans watched the ____________ match.

The ____________ racer across the finish line was the ____________ student.

The writer's purpose is to tell the reader about her grandfather's trip.

Giant Pandas

My lucky grandpa went on a fabulous trip to China last month. He came back with photos of his visit with giant pandas in Chengdu. I really love his panda photos. The pandas look so soft and cuddly. They are huge. Grandpa said he had to wash his hands and wear a surgical gown and gloves, like a doctor, so that he didn't give the pandas germs. He fed carrots to one panda and held it in his lap while it ate. I would really love to go to Chengdu one day to see the pandas.

By Olivia

1. Read *Giant Pandas*. Underline the **proper nouns**.

2. Write three **describing adjectives** for what the pandas looked like.

   ______________________ ______________________ ______________________

3. Circle the **pronoun** *he* in the text. Which **noun** does *he* replace? ______________________

4. Find four words from the text that let readers know Olivia's opinion about things. They might be **adjectives** (*scary, loving, gorgeous, kind*) or **verbs** (*hate, avoid*).

   ______________________ ______________________

   ______________________ ______________________

5. If Olivia had a conversation with a friend, what might she say about Grandpa's trip? Use **quoted speech**.

   ____

   ____

6 Circle the **noun groups**.

I saw six fat piglets.

Emily looked at the three Siamese kittens.

We ate five delicious chocolate chip cookies.

Arthur collected 25 aluminium cans.

Tip Remember the rule about **noun groups** on page 41.

7 Add an **adjective** from the box to complete each **noun group**.

muddy old five new beach

Billy owns __________ goldfish.

Gran collects __________ stamps.

The dog had __________ feet.

They have photos of a __________ holiday.

We are moving to a __________ house.

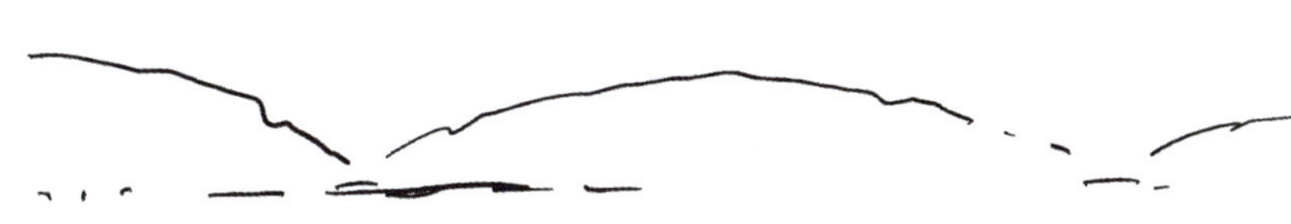

8 Use a **conjunction** (*or, so, but, and*) to join the **clauses** on each line.

Pandas mainly eat bamboo __________ they also like carrots.

Grandpa wore gloves __________ he would not give the pandas germs.

Olivia's mother hopes to go to China __________ Olivia's stepfather does not want to go to China.

Grandpa might go to New Zealand next, __________ he could go to Fiji.

Write how you feel about something that is special to you. Describe its features using **noun groups**.

Unit 20 Questions and statements

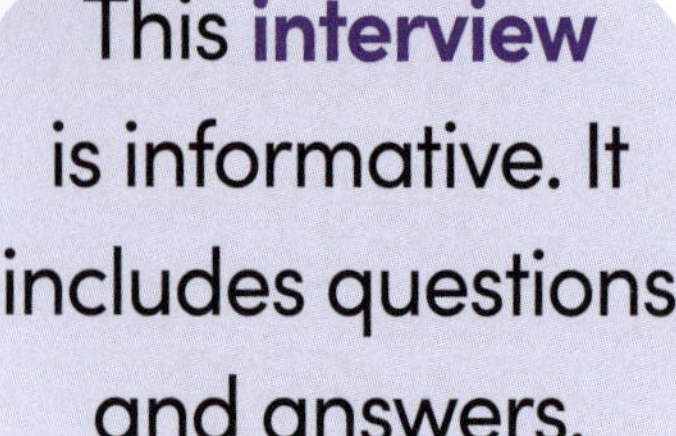

Wildlife Carer

A wildlife carer visited our school. These are some questions we asked, and her answers.

What kinds of animals do you look after?

I look after any sick, injured or orphaned native animals. I often care for native birds and possums.

How do you know what to do for the animals?

I had training. Plus there is a buddy system. When you first become an animal carer you are matched with someone with more experience than you. My buddy helped me a lot.

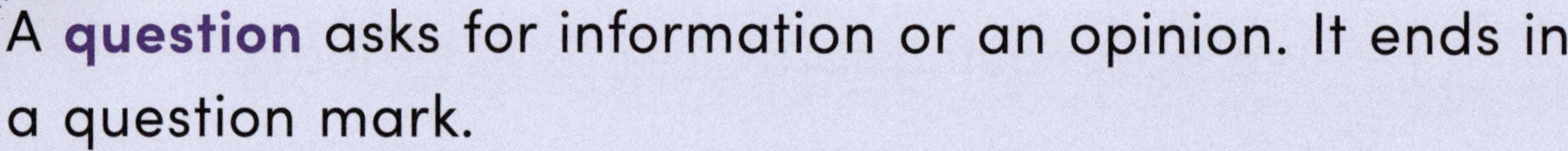

Rule A **question** asks for information or an opinion. It ends in a question mark.
What is a Welcome to Country? Can he play the didgeridoo?

1 Read *Wildlife Carer.* Underline the two **questions**.

2 Write three **questions** you would ask a wildlife carer in an interview.

____

____

____

Rule A **statement** can be a **fact**. *Polar bears live at the North Pole.*
A **statement** can give an **opinion**. *Polar bear cubs are cute.*
Statements end in a full stop.

3 Answer the **question** with a **statement** that gives your **opinion**.
Would you like to be a wildlife carer? Why or why not?

____

____

Grammar Rules! Student Book 2 (ISBN 9780655092421) © Tanya Gibb/Matilda Education Australia

4 Write the possum's answer.

5 Write the pelican's answer.

6 Tick a column to show whether each **statement** gives a **fact** or an **opinion**.

	Fact	Opinion
Dogs have four legs.	______	______
Lucy is scared of dogs.	______	______
Wombats are mammals.	______	______
I love wombats.	______	______

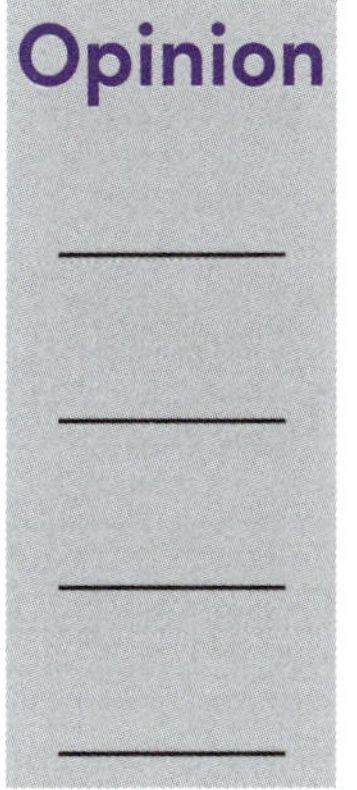

7 Write a **fact** about the spider picture.

____

Write an **opinion** about the spider picture.

____

Work with a partner. **Interview** a student or teacher at your school. Ask them three **questions** about their favourite animal. Write the **questions** and their answers.

Reflection

 I can do this.

 I am not sure.

 I need help.

This text is informative. It tells about a Gundungurra Dreaming story that explains how the land was formed.

How The Land was Formed

The area around the Blue Mountains is on Gundungurra country. The land was carved out when two giant ancestral spirits had a big battle. One was the giant Gurangatch, part-snake and part-fish. The other was the giant Mirrangan, a quoll.

Their battle began when Mirrangan tried to catch Gurangatch to eat. Gurangatch escaped, burrowing into the earth and carving out great caves, tunnels and rivers. Mirrangan ran above the ground, digging deep holes to try to reach Gurangatch underground.

Gurangatch managed to escape but is still hiding in the waters on Gundungurra country.

1 Read *How the Land was Formed.* What landforms did the two giant ancestor spirits make?

________________ ________________ ________________

2 What kind of animal was Mirrangan? ________________

3 What kind of animal was Gurangatch? ________________

4 Where does Gurangatch live? ________________

5 Underline the **proper nouns** in *How the Land was Formed.*

6 Complete these **noun groups** from *How the Land was Formed.*

two ________ ________ spirits ________ tunnels

________ holes ________ caves a ________ battle

Grammar Rules! Student Book 2 (ISBN 9780655092421) © Tanya Gibb/Matilda Education Australia

7 Write **action verbs** from the box to complete the sentences.

dug	burrowed	carved	chased

Gurangatch ______________ underground through the earth.

Gurangatch ______________ out great caves, tunnels and rivers.

Mirrangan ______________ Gurangatch.

Mirrangan ______________ deep holes.

8 Write the correct **article** (*a, an, the*) on each line. If the article starts a sentence, it needs an **upper-case letter**.

______ quoll is a small, meat-eating marsupial.

Quolls are under threat in ______ wild.

______ Eastern Quoll is now extinct on mainland Australia.

9 Use a **conjunction** from the box to join the **clauses** in each sentence.

and	so	but	or

Mirrangan had to escape ______ he would have been eaten.

Gurangatch carved out tunnels ______ Mirrangan dug big holes.

Gurangatch loves the water ______ Mirrangan does not like to swim.

The story of Mirrangan and Gurangatch is told ______ that people know how the land was formed.

10 Circle the **compound words** in *How the Land was Formed.*

Find and read an Australian First Nations Dreaming story. Retell it in your own words to a friend or a class group. Use volume, pace and emphasis to engage your audience.

This narrative is a modern version of the nursery rhyme *Little Miss Muffet.*

Along Came a Spider

Once upon a time Millie Muffet was sitting in her bedroom listening to music when all of sudden a spider dropped from the ceiling next to her. Millie Muffet jumped up off her chair.

"Oh!" she cried. "You poor little thing! Did you hurt yourself? You don't belong in here. Let me help you."

Millie Muffet kindly took the spider in her hands and set it free out the back door.

1 Read *Along Came a Spider.* Write the words used that often begin a nursery rhyme.

____

2 Where must Millie think the spider belongs? ______________________________

3 Underline the **quoted speech** in *Along Came a Spider.*

4 Write two **adjectives** that could describe the spider. ______________ ______________

5 Write four **adjectives** of your own to describe Millie's behaviour.

______________ ______________ ______________ ______________

6 Write the **pronouns** that refer to Millie Muffet in *Along Came a Spider.*

______________ ______________

7 Write the **question** from *Along Came a Spider.*

____

Grammar Rules! Student Book 2 (ISBN 9780655092421) © Tanya Gibb/Matilda Education Australia

8 How can you tell that *Along Came a Spider* is set in modern times?

___

9 Circle the **exclamations** in *Along Came a Spider.*

10 Write an **exclamation** for what you would say if you saw the spider.

___

11 Write an **exclamation** in **quoted speech** for each situation.

Marty breaks a glass. ___

Prisha gets a great birthday gift. ___

Zac thought a First Nations dance performance was deadly.

___

Natalia is about to step on broken glass but Riku warns her.

___

12 Use a full stop, a question mark or an exclamation mark at the end of each **sentence**. Tick the correct column.

	Statement	Question	Exclamation
I need to clean the birdcage	___	___	___
Sam, clean the birdcage	___	___	___
Can we go to the concert	___	___	___
Wow	___	___	___
Alinta is a great slam poet	___	___	___

Try it yourself!

Choose a nursery rhyme such as *Little Bo Peep Has Lost Her Sheep* or *Jack and Jill Went Up the Hill.* Write a modern-day **narrative** version.

Reflection

I can do this.

I am not sure.

I need help.

Unit 23

Emotive words, exclamations, questions

The writer's purpose in this **advertisement** is to sell three llamas.

Llamas for Sale

Beautiful brown eyes, long eyelashes, gentle and friendly.

How can you resist?

Llamas **NEEDING GOOD HOMES**

Today only! Three Llamas for $300.

All they need now is a good owner and a large paddock.

Also – for a limited time only – three bales of hay, as well as a llama brush, free with all sales.

So, what are you waiting for?

This fabulous offer is for today only **so don't miss out!**

(NB: Llamas not sold separately.)

1 Read *Llamas for Sale.* Write the **noun group** that describes the llamas' eyes.

____

2 Write a **noun group** that could describe a suitable home for a llama.

____

3 Write two **questions** from the text.

____

4 Write the **exclamation** from the text that is a compound sentence.

____

____

5 Why might the llamas need new homes? Write three possible reasons.

____

____

____

Rule

Emotive words appeal to emotions. They are used in advertisements to persuade people to buy something.

Don't miss out! *Fabulous offer!*

6 Underline the **emotive words** in *Llamas for Sale.* These are all the words that might convince you to buy the llamas.

7 *Llamas for Sale* uses the **emotive words** *Don't miss out.* How do you feel when you miss out on something that you really want?

____

____

8 Tick the sentence in each pair that most makes you want to buy something.

☐	You will love these.	☐	You might like these.
☐	You must get one.	☐	Maybe get one.
☐	It's a little bit friendly.	☐	It's very friendly and lovable.
☐	Offer only on today.	☐	No offers available.
☐	Lazy and stubborn.	☐	Intelligent and easy to train.

9 Complete the sentence.

Llamas are lovable because ______________________________.

Try it yourself!

Write an **advertisement** for a pet. It can be a real pet or a pretend pet. Write the pet's breed. Describe what it looks like. Describe its habits. Use **emotive words** that will persuade someone to buy it.

Reflection

- I can do this.
- I am not sure.
- I need help.

Unit 24 Revision

1 Write a sentence for each **personal pronoun** in the box.

he she it they I

____

____

____

____

____

2 Underline the **noun groups**.

The llama has lovely brown eyes.

The friendly llamas stood together.

Llama farms produce llama wool.

The scarf was made of soft llama wool.

3 Tick a column to show whether the statement gives a **fact** or an **opinion**.

	Fact	Opinion
Llamas have ears.	______	______
Llamas are beautiful.	______	______
Echidnas are friendly.	______	______
Female kangaroos have pouches.	______	______
Wombats dig.	______	______

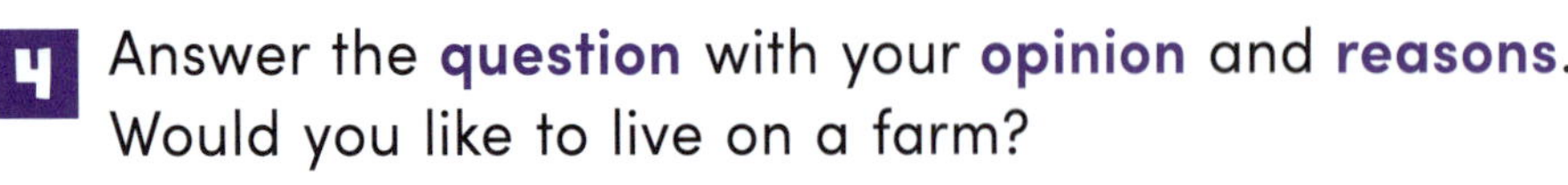

4 Answer the **question** with your **opinion** and **reasons**.
Would you like to live on a farm?

____

____

5 Imagine you are going to buy three llamas. Write two **questions** to ask the person selling the llamas.

____

____

6 Use each word in the box in a sentence as part of a prepositional phrase.

over	______________________________
around	______________________________
behind	______________________________
between	______________________________

7 Rewrite each sentence with correct punctuation.

do you like hermit crabs

____

I think hermit crabs are interesting said lila

____

8 Add a **conjunction** to each sentence.

Tasha likes llamas __________ Nico does not like llamas at all.

Tasha likes llamas __________ Lev likes llamas, too.

Gisele likes llamas __________ she lives on a farm __________ she can buy some llamas.

9 Tick the sentence in each pair that most makes you want to buy something.

- [ ] I think you'll want one.
- [ ] I know you'll want one.
- [ ] You must have one.
- [ ] Maybe you should get one.
- [ ] It's quite cute.
- [ ] It's absolutely gorgeous.

Unit 25 Paragraphs, reported speech, apostrophes for possession

The writer's purpose is to present different opinions about zoos.

Zoos

Zoos are popular places to visit but is it 'right' to keep wild animals in cages?

Some people believe that zoos are cruel. These people think that animals should live in their natural habitat in the wild.

Other people say that zoos do an important job. Zoos study animals to learn more about helping them survive. Zoos also try to breed endangered animals. Then, if they do disappear from the wild, at least they can survive in zoos.

I think zoos do a good job of teaching people about animals. I think zoos are necessary.

Rule A **paragraph** is a sentence or a number of sentences based on the same idea. A paragraph begins on a new line.

1 Read *Zoos*. Summarise the main idea of each **paragraph**.

Paragraph 1: Introduction	Paragraph 2: One point of view
______ ______ ______	______ ______ ______
Paragraph 3: Different point of view	**Paragraph 4: Summing up**
______ ______ ______	______ ______ ______

Grammar Rules! Student Book 2 (ISBN 9780655092421) © Tanya Gibb/Matilda Education Australia

Rule **Reported speech** is not quoted in quotation marks.
Reported speech: *Jai said that he loves the gorillas at the zoo.*
Quoted speech: *Jai said, "I love the gorillas at the zoo."*

2 Rewrite each sentence as **reported speech**.

Kathryn said, "Monkeys are funny."

____

Eliza commented, "Orangutans are funnier."

____

"Chimpanzees are the funniest," said Mohammed.

____

3 Rewrite each sentence as **quoted speech**.

Toby agreed that it's cruel to keep whales in zoos.

____

Suri said that she loves watching the otters.

____

Rule An **apostrophe** can be used before an *s* to show possession.
In a **plural noun**, the apostrophe goes after the *s*.
Paolo's jumper *the dog's bone* *the students' books*

4 Rewrite the sentence correctly.

have you seen mayas homework book asked felix

____

What do people at your school think about zoos? Interview adults and students. Write a **discussion** to present the points of view. Use **reported speech** to report what people said.

How Do Penguin Chicks Eat?

Many birds regurgitate food for their chicks to eat. This is a bit like vomiting.

There are three ways that penguin chicks can be fed. It depends on what species they are.

1. The parent swallows the fish. It travels to the penguin's stomach. Here, a special chemical stops the fish from being digested. A few days later the parent regurgitates the fish for the chick. The fish is as fresh as ever.
2. The parents partly digest their fishy food. Then they regurgitate slop into their chick's mouth.
3. The parent totally digests the fish. The fish then turns into very rich oil. The parent feeds this to the chick.

Do you have a pet bird? Has it ever regurgitated some of its food onto you? That means it loves you very much.

This **explanation** is informative. Its purpose is to explain how penguin chicks eat.

Rule

Words in a **noun group** can:

- point out *that penguin chick*
  these those that
- show ownership *their baby*
  his her their your my our its

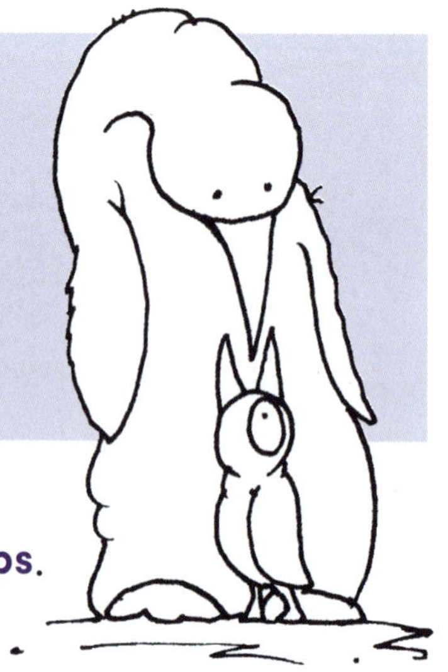

1 Read *How Do Penguin Chicks Eat?* Underline any four **noun groups**.

2 Underline the **noun group** in each sentence.

We won't eat these squishy old bananas.

My little puppy watched us.

Those monkeys are sleeping.

That monkey is cheekiest.

3 Draw a diagram with arrows to show the sequence in step 1 of *How do Penguin Chicks Eat?* Label each box.

4 Add a **prepositional phrase** from the box to complete each simple sentence.

with scaly skin	on blood	from a flower
into the chick's mouth	on its underside	

The parent penguin regurgitates food ______________________.

An octopus's mouth is ______________________.

A vampire bat feeds ______________________.

A hummingbird sucks nectar ______________________.

A reptile is a cold-blooded animal ______________________.

5 Write a **question** about penguins beginning with each question word.

Who ______________________

When ______________________

Where ______________________

How ______________________

Try it yourself!

Write an **explanation**. You might choose to explain why bats hang upside down or why a cow's stomach has four sections. Write your explanation in a logical sequence.

Reflection

- I can do this.
- I am not sure.
- I need help.

Reptile Encounter

Last Monday my class went on an excursion to see reptiles.

Firstly we saw an eastern blue-tongue. It mainly eats snails. It felt very smooth. Then we saw a shingleback. It has a short round tail, which predators think is its head. It's rough and bumpy-looking. Flowers are its favourite food. After that we saw crocodiles and snakes. Lastly we saw a number of different kinds of geckoes. They can all be found in Australia.

I learned a lot about reptiles on that excursion.

The writer's purpose is to inform readers about events that have happened and give an opinion.

1 Read *Reptile Encounter*. Underline the **noun groups** that name four kinds of reptiles.

2 Circle the **time connectives** in *Reptile Encounter*.

Apostrophes can be used in a shortened form of a word or words. They show that one or more letters have been left out. Shortened words are called **contractions**.

*she's → she **is*** *I've → I **ha**ve*

3 Write the word in *Reptile Encounter* that is a **contraction**. ____________________

4 Draw lines to link the **contractions** to the full words.

I'll	he is
he's	we will
you're	I will
we'll	you are
I'm	they have
they've	I am
could've	cannot
can't	could have

Rule

A **dependent clause** depends on a **main clause** to make complete sense. **Conjunctions** link dependent clauses.

that whether while after when because if

A comma separates a dependent clause from a main clause when the dependent clause comes first.

Dependent clause *After we saw the snakes and crocodiles,*
Main clause (independent clause) *we saw the geckoes.*

4 Draw a line from each **dependent clause** to a **main clause** to complete the sentences.

After she saw the blue-tongue,	Freya saw the crocodiles get fed.
Whenever we visit the reptile park,	Freya visited the blue-tongues first.
Because she loves blue-tongues,	Freya saw a shingleback.
Unless the bus arrives soon,	we are allowed to touch some reptiles.
While she was watching them,	we'll be late back to school.

5 Circle the **dependent clauses** below. Underline the **verbs** first to help identify each clause.

While he was waiting for Uncle, Max saw a blue-tongue lizard. It was sitting on a rock while the sun was out. When Max moved closer, the blue-tongue scurried away. While it hid, Max left some banana on the rock.

Write a **recount** of a trip or excursion you have had. Write what you did and what you saw. End with an **opinion**. Use different kinds of sentences to make your writing interesting.

28 Subject–verb agreement, alliteration, rhyme

This recipe for a magic potion is imaginative. Its purpose is to entertain.

"Talk to the Animals" Potion

WARNING! THIS MAGIC POTION IS VERY DANGEROUS.

Only use a little bit.

Ingredients

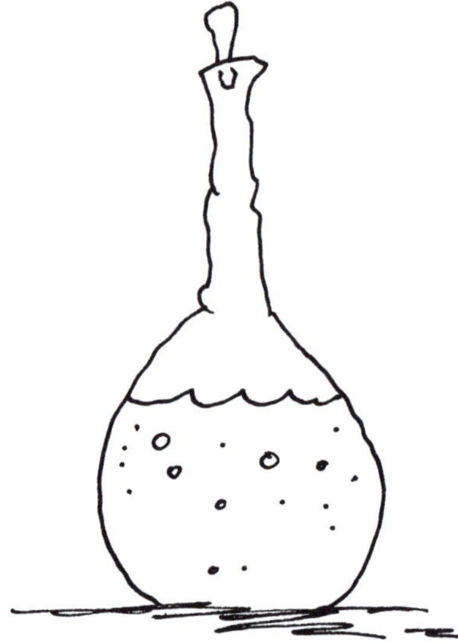

1 empty snail shell
4 flamingo feathers
11 leaves off a lemon tree
5 pink petunia petals
3 thimbles of thistledown
6 cups cow cream

Method

1. Grind shell, feathers, leaves and petals.
2. Mix all ingredients together.
3. Apply to skin. Leave on for 24 hours.
4. Dance the "cha-cha" and chant three times:
   "Animal lingo ling-gwistic ling-gwini la la."
5. Rinse the potion off in the ocean.

WARNING: If animal voices sound weird, you need to use the magic remedy.

1 Work with a partner. Read *"Talk to the Animals" Potion* out loud together. Practise the chant in step 4 of the method.

2 Circle the **action verbs** in *"Talk to the Animals" Potion.*

3 Write five **action verbs** of your own that can be found in recipes.

Rule

Alliteration is when sounds are repeated at the beginning of words. *Greedy Godfrey glugged and gurgled till it was gone.*
Rhyme is when the ends of words sound the same.

catch *scratch* *patch*

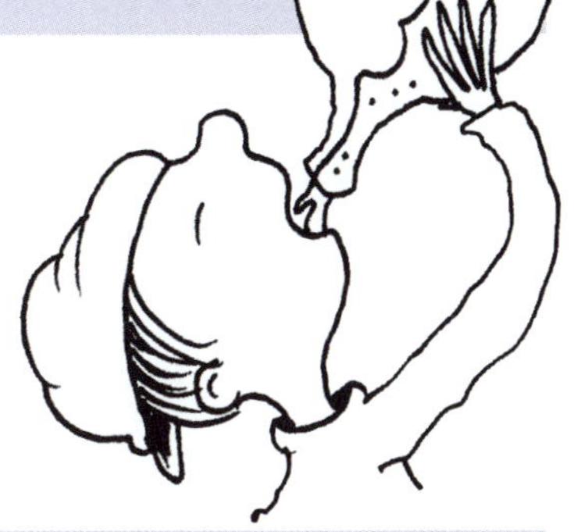

4 Underline the **alliteration** in *"Talk to the Animals" Potion.*

5 Write the two words that **rhyme** in *"Talk to the Animals" Potion.*

____________________ ____________________

Rule

Subject (**noun** or **pronoun**) and **verb** have to agree in number.

	Subject	**Verb**
Correct	We	are waiting.
Incorrect	We	is waiting.

6 Circle the correct **verb** on each line.

Everyone | like | likes | to talk to animals.

Flamingo feathers | is | are | needed for the recipe.

Finding an empty snail shell | is | are | difficult.

Using the recipe | is | are | a good idea.

Marion and Denzel | is | are | good cooks.

Marie | lives | live | in Kellyville.

7 Imagine you are going to sell the *"Talk to the Animals"* potion. Use paper to create a label for a jar of the potion. Use **emotive words** to persuade people to buy your potion.

Try it yourself!

If someone uses too much of the *"Talk to the Animals"* potion, they need to take a magic remedy. Write a **recipe** for the magic remedy. Use **rhyme** and **alliteration**.

Reflection

I can do this.

I am not sure.

I need help.

Unit **29** Topic sentences, subject–verb agreement, prepositional phrases

This text is informative. It is an **information report** about ringtail possums.

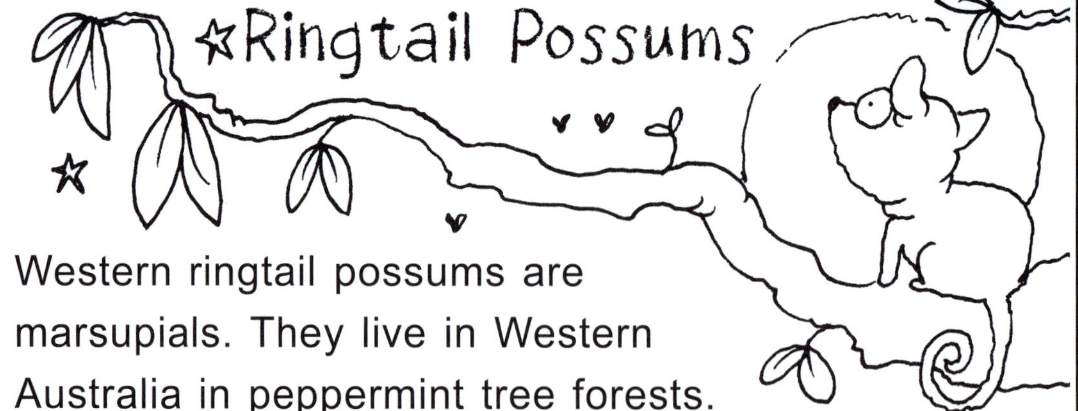

Ringtail Possums

Western ringtail possums are marsupials. They live in Western Australia in peppermint tree forests.

A western ringtail possum has distinctive fur. It is brown with creamy-white fur on its chest and stomach. It has a white tip on its really long tail. It uses its tail to climb trees and carry nesting materials.

Western ringtail possums are active at night. They sleep during the day and live in family groups.

Western ringtails are dying due to habitat loss. They are also killed by cats, dogs, foxes and cars. The possums are in danger of extinction.

1 Read *Ringtail Possums*. Underline the **noun** *possums*. Circle the **personal pronouns**.

2 Add a **preposition** from the box to complete each sentence.

with	at	in	during	by	inside

Look ___________ that huge peppermint tree.

The possum nest is ___________ the hollow of the tree.

Possum nests are lined ___________ leaves.

Sit ___________ the tree.

Keep cats ___________ the house ___________ the night.

3 Write the items in the sequence that uses commas in *Ringtail Possums.*

The **topic sentence** of a paragraph is often the first sentence. It tells what the paragraph is about.

4 Write the **topic sentence** of each paragraph in *Ringtail Possums.*

Paragraph 1 ______

Paragraph 2 ______

Paragraph 3 ______

Paragraph 4 ______

5 Write six **prepositional phrases** from *Ringtail Possums.*

6 Circle the **verb** that agrees with the **subject** in each sentence.

Western ringtails | live | lives | in peppermint forests.

The possum | has | have | white fur on its belly.

The possums | sleeps | sleep | during the day.

They | is | are | active at night.

The possum | uses | use | its tail when climbing.

Find out about an Australian animal. Write a **report**. Write paragraphs telling where it lives, what it looks like and what it does.

Reflection

I can do this.

I am not sure.

I need help.

Unit 30

Revision

1 Circle the correct **verb** for the **subject** in each clause.

Nazeem | lives | live | in Hobart.

Everyone I know | like | likes | ice cream.

Mushrooms | is | are | needed for the recipe.

My dog | is | are | hard to train.

Using that blunt knife | is | are | not a good idea.

Jo says she | did | does | not like Brussels sprouts.

2 Rewrite each sentence as **quoted speech**.

Pamela said she's worried about ringtail possums.

____

John said he's worried too.

____

Riku thinks that foxes are the worst threat to ringtails.

____

3 Circle the **topic sentence** in the paragraph.

Assistance dogs can help people with physical disabilities by picking up dropped items, opening doors, retrieving the phone, emergency barking and also by just being a companion. Assistance dogs are trained to help people.

4 Circle the **dependent clause** in each sentence.

Because you're running late, we'll go ahead.

Don't take the camera unless you are going to use it.

While walking in the park, Tara found a lost dog.

Although he is good at maths, Sajid did not finish his maths test.

You love crocodiles so go see them first.

Every time I go to the beach, I use sunscreen.

5 Rewrite each **noun group** by adding the **possessive apostrophe**.

the cats nose ______________________

all the students books

____

Uncle Ivans recipe

____

each students book

____

6 Draw a line to link each **contraction** to the full words.

should've	she is
she's	you will
you'll	do not
don't	could have
I'm	must not
mustn't	I am
could've	should have

7 What is the writer's purpose in each text? Write your answers on the lines.

Buy now! This great deal on soccer balls won't last.

____

Last Saturday, I went to the park with my friends. First we had fun on the equipment. Then we played with a soccer ball. After that we had lunch. ______________________

Sea lions can move quickly on land and in the water.

____

Unit 31 Clauses, conjunctions

Corroboree Frogs

The southern corroboree frog of Australia is almost extinct. It only lives in a small area of the Snowy Mountains in New South Wales.

Southern corroboree frogs have bright yellow stripes on a black body. The adult frogs are only tiny. They are just over two centimetres long.

Frogs lay eggs. Eggs hatch into tadpoles. The tadpoles of the southern corroboree frog change into frogs when they are one year old. They grow back legs first and then front legs. Then their tails disappear and they become froglets.

This text is informative. It tells where the frogs live, what they look like and about their life cycle.

1 Read *Corroboree Frogs*. Circle the **personal pronouns**.

2 Draw a cycle diagram on a piece of paper to show how frog eggs become frogs. Label your diagram. Use words and phrases from *Corroboree Frogs*.

3 Use a **relating verb** from the box to complete each sentence.

am	is	have	has	are

Frogs ________ amphibians.

Frogs ________ cold blood.

I ________ interested in frogs.

A froglet ________ a tiny tail stump.

A corroboree frog egg ________ like a marble.

Grammar Rules! Student Book 2 (ISBN 9780655092421) © Tanya Gibb/Matilda Education Australia

A **subordinating conjunction** (*while, after, if, when, because, although, since*) links a **dependent clause** to a **main clause** in complex sentences.

4 Circle the **subordinating conjunctions** and underline the **dependent clauses**.

While they are not extinct, there is hope for the survival of southern corroboree frogs.

Although time for action is running out, there is hope for corroboree frogs.

Because it only lives at the top of mountains, the frog is under threat from climate change.

When they are one year old, the tadpoles change into frogs.

The frog species is never going to survive unless there's action on climate change.

The frog grows a tail after it has grown four legs.

5 Underline a sentence in *Corroboree Frogs* that uses a subordinating clause.

6 Add commas where necessary.

Corroboree frog tadpoles eat beetles bugs ants insect larvae and mites. Adult corroboree frogs eat ants beetles and mites.

Find out about an endangered animal that interests you. Make a class book of **information reports**. Write what the animal looks like, where it lives, what it eats and why it is endangered.

The Chimp and the Crocodile

Once upon a time there lived a small chimpanzee. The chimp's name was Charlie.

One day, Charlie was playing on a branch that hung over a lake. Suddenly, the branch snapped. Charlie fell into the lake. Charlie could swim a little bit but not very far. He started to sink into the deep water.

All of a sudden he was lifted to the surface. He took a big gulp of air. A crocodile had saved his life.

The crocodile's name was Winifred. She was a vegetarian. Apples were her favourite food. Charlie decided to collect an enormous basket of apples and other sweet fruit for Winifred every week to thank her.

Charlie and Winifred stayed best friends forever.

This imaginative text is a **narrative** in the form of a modern-day fable.

1 Read *The Chimp and the Crocodile*. Use words from *The Chimp and the Crocodile* to write what is happening in each drawing.

1. ______ ______ ______	2. ______ ______ ______
3. ______ ______ ______	4. ______ ______ ______

Grammar Rules! Student Book 2 (ISBN 9780655092421) © Tanya Gibb/Matilda Education Australia

2 Who is the main character in the story? ____________________

3 Circle the **proper nouns** in *The Chimp and the Crocodile*.

Rule

The tense of a **verb** helps tell when an event happens. Events are either happening now, they happened in the past or they will happen in the future.

past *The frog hopped yesterday.*

present *The frog is hopping now.*

future *The frog will hop tomorrow.*

4 Complete each sentence. Find **verbs** in *The Chimp and the Crocodile* to tell that events happened in the **past**.

There ____________ a small chimpanzee.

The chimp ____________ on a branch.

The branch ____________.

Charlie was ____________ to the surface.

A crocodile had ____________ his life.

Charlie ____________ to get a basket of fruit.

5 Use a **verb** from the box to complete each sentence.

swam
saved
looked
fell

The chimpanzee ____________ into the water.

The crocodile ____________ Charlie.

The crocodile ____________ to the rescue.

The birds in the trees ____________ on.

Try it yourself!

The Chimp and the Crocodile is a form of **narrative** that is called a fable. Fables have morals. The moral of this fable is 'one good turn deserves another'. Write a fable. Write the moral at the end of your fable.

Reflection

I can do this.

I am not sure.

I need help.

Unit 33

Instructions, subject–verb agreement

These **instructions** are informative. They tell how to look after a pet.

HOW TO LOOK AFTER A TARANTULA

Your tarantula will need:

A house: This can be a fish tank. Cover the floor of the tank with potting mix. Then add leaf litter and bark.

A heating device: Keep the temperature of the tank between 21 and 24°C.

Water: Provide drinking water in a small dish. The lid of a jar will do.

Food: Tarantulas eat crickets, cockroaches, moths and caterpillars.

Care: Tarantulas moult (shed their skin) a few times a year. Mostly they turn onto their backs to moult. They lie still for a few hours. Do not handle your tarantula. You could hurt it. Tarantulas stop eating before a moult. Stop feeding your tarantula during its moult. The live food might bite it. Tarantulas do not need food for 4–5 days when their new skin has hardened.

1 Read *How to Look After a Tarantula.* List the five key things a pet tarantula needs.

____

2 Write a **proper noun** for the name you would choose for a tarantula. ______________

3 Write seven **plural nouns** used in *How to Look After a Tarantula.*

Remember the **plural nouns** rule on page 38.

____

____

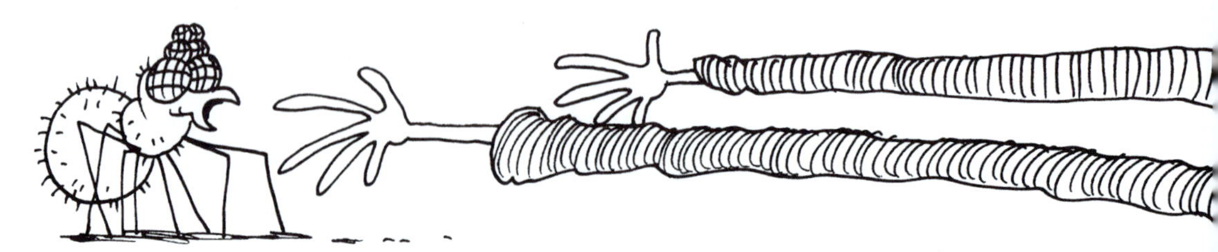

Grammar Rules! Student Book 2 (ISBN 9780655092421) © Tanya Gibb/Matilda Education Australia

4 Circle the correct **verb** in each **sentence**.

Tarantulas | likes | like | a temperature of 21–24 °C.

Your tarantula | need | needs | a water dish.

My tarantula | eat | eats | cockroaches.

Tarantulas | moults | moult | a few times a year.

If your tarantula | are | is | on its back, it's probably moulting.

5 Circle the **verb** in each **sentence**. Then tick the **sentences** that are **instructions**.

Tarantulas shed their exoskeleton.

Cover the tank with potting mix.

Add leaves and bark.

Feed your tarantula crickets.

I love my tarantula.

6 Unscramble each **instruction**. Write the instructions on the lines.

give spider water the ____________________

food feed the spider live ____________________

tank keep the warm ____________________

your tarantula watch moult ____________________

fish tank use a ____________________

Write a set of **instructions** that tells how to care for an animal or an imaginary pet. It could be a pet you have or a pet you would like to have. Use **action verbs** to tell what to do.

Unit 34 Conjunctions, clauses

How Sea Animals Breathe

Whales are mammals. They breathe air just like humans. Humans and whales need the oxygen in the air. Whales have one or two nostrils on top of their heads. These nostrils are called blowholes. The whale comes to the surface and blows out all its used air. Used air is air with no oxygen left in it. Then the whale breathes in fresh air. Now it can dive again.

Fish breathe oxygen too. Their oxygen is dissolved in the water. Fish have sets of flat gills on both sides of their mouths. A fish sucks water into its mouth then pushes the water back out through its gills. As the water flows past the gills, the gills pick up all the oxygen. This is how fish breathe under water.

This text is informative. It **explains** how sea animals breathe.

1 Read *How Sea Animals Breathe.* Draw and label how whales breathe. Draw and label how fish breathe.

Whales	Fish
Breathe out	Breathe in
Breathe in	Breathe out

2 In *How Sea Animals Breathe*, underline three **action verbs** that whales do.

3 In *How Sea Animals Breathe*, circle three **action verbs** that fish do.

4 Draw lines to join the parts of the **sentences**. Hint! The underlined **conjunctions** will help you join correctly.

Because whales are mammals,	then it breathes in fresh air.
Humans are mammals	but they don't breathe air.
The whale breathes out used air	they need to breathe air.
Fish need oxygen	so they need to breathe air.
Whales need to surface	otherwise they will die.
Animals need oxygen	so that they can breathe.

5 Complete each **sentence** with a **conjunction** from the box.
If the conjunction begins the sentence, use an **upper-case letter**.

after	while	because	since

__________ you were shopping, I finished my book.

__________ her shoes were too tight, Amelia got blisters.

You can watch television __________ you have done your homework.

__________ you won't help me, I'll do it myself.

6 Join the simple sentences. Rewrite the new sentences.

My soup had gone cold. I heated it in the microwave.

____

Theo returned the shirt to the shop. He noticed it had a stain.

____

Find out how humans breathe. How do we get oxygen out of the air? Write an **explanation**. Or, draw a series of diagrams to explain how we breathe. Label your diagrams.

Unit 35 Revision

1 Circle the **noun groups** and **pronouns** that refer to the hermit crab.

I couldn't find my hermit crab. It had escaped from its tank. I looked in my bedroom. I looked in the kitchen and in the bathroom. I looked in the lounge room. I found it in the laundry. It was hiding under a wet mop.

2 Circle the **prepositional phrases**. The phrases all tell ______________________________

I couldn't find my hermit crab. It had escaped from its tank. I looked in my bedroom. I looked in the kitchen and in the bathroom. I looked in the lounge room. I found it in the laundry. It was hiding under a wet mop.

3 Circle the correct **verb** in each sentence.

Hermit crabs | has | have | shells.

A corroboree frog | has | have | yellow stripes.

I | are | am | interested in spiders.

They | love | loves | to swim.

He | sing | sings | to the baby.

4 Rewrite each sentence with correct punctuation.

taronga zoo is collecting frogs eggs said finn

____

is the zoo trying to help the frogs asked ariana

____

5 Write a **proper noun** to name a baby dinosaur. ______________________________

Grammar Rules! Student Book 2 (ISBN 9780655092421) © Tanya Gibb/Matilda Education Australia

6 Circle the correct **verb** to show the action was in the past.

I | played | play | recorder in the concert last night.

Dad | work | worked | all yesterday, painting the fence.

Mum is | mowing | mowed | the lawn this morning.

I | help | helped | Katrina earlier.

My sister | makes | made | mud pies after breakfast.

7 Circle the **verb** in each **sentence**. Tick the sentences that are **instructions**.

Hermit crabs swap shells.

Buy extra shells for the tank.

Touch your hermit crabs gently.

Hermit crabs run quickly.

Clean your hermit crab tank.

8 Unscramble and rewrite the **sentences** correctly. Use **upper-case letters** and full stops.

chickens from hatch eggs ______________________________

go with aunty Ill ______________________________

for the spider out watch ______________________________

the magpies nesting are ______________________________

9 Draw lines to join the **clauses** correctly. Hint! The underlined **conjunctions** wlll help you join correctly.

<u>Because</u> we need milk,	<u>then</u> I'll pack the picnic basket.
We'll take the dog too,	<u>but</u> we probably won't need them.
I'll make sandwiches	I'll walk to the shop.
We'll take raincoats	<u>so that</u> we can sit on the ground.
We'll take a blanket	<u>otherwise</u> she'll be upset.

Glossary

Look at the page number in the circle to find more information about the rule or tip.

adjective .... a word that tells you more about a **noun** (21)

quantity adjective (41)

adverb .... a word that adds meaning to a **verb**, **adjective** or another **adverb**

adding meaning to ***verbs*** *by telling how* (39)

alliteration .... when sounds are repeated at the beginning of words (63)

antonym .... a word that means the opposite to another word (23)

apostrophe .... a punctuation mark

used to show possession (57) *used in a contraction* (60)

article .... a small word (*a*, *an*, *the*) used in front of a **noun** or at the start of a **noun group** (41)

clause .... a group of words that includes a **verb**

a ***simple sentence*** *is one clause* (11) (14)

a ***main clause*** *(independent clause) is a complete message* (61)

a ***dependent clause*** *(subordinate clause) adds meaning to a main clause and depends on a main clause to make a complete message* (61) (69)

subject *of a clause* (14)

comma .... a punctuation mark that separates:

words in a series (12)

quoted speech *(direct speech) in dialogue* (17)

a ***dependent clause*** *from a* ***main clause*** *when the dependent clause is written first in the sentence* (61)

command .... a sentence that tells someone to do something (32)

compound word .. a word formed by combining two other words (35)

conjunction .... a word that connects words, phrases or **clauses** (24) (69)

coordinating conjunction (24) (61) (69)

subordinating conjunction (61) (69)

emotive word ...... a word that appeals to the emotions (53)

exclamation .... a sentence that shows strong emotion, or gives a warning or command (16)

noun .... a word for a person, place, animal or thing

common noun *and* ***proper nouns*** (9)

noun group (41) (58)

singular *and* ***plural*** (38)

Grammar Rules! Student Book 2 (ISBN 9780655092421) © Tanya Gibb/Matilda Education Australia

onomatopoeia.....the name given to words that sound like the things they represent 29

paragraph............a sentence or a number of sentences based on the same idea. A paragraph begins on a new line. 56

topic sentence often the first sentence; tells what the paragraph is about 65

personal pronoun.................a word that is used in place of a **noun** 33

preposition...........a word that shows the relationship between a **noun** or **pronoun** and another word 27

prepositional phrase...................a unit of meaning that begins with a **preposition**

a phrase can tell where or when 27

question................a **sentence** that asks for information or an opinion 46

quoted speech.....the actual speech someone says; uses quotation marks 17 57

reported speech...speech that is not quoted directly 57

rhyme......................when the ends of words sound the same 63

sentence................a group of words that makes sense on its own. It must include at least one **verb**.

simple 11

compound 24

complex 69

statement of fact or opinion 46

statement..............a **sentence** that gives a fact or an opinion 46

subject–verb agreement............the subject (**noun** or **pronoun**) and **verb** have to agree in number 63

synonym.................a word that has a similar meaning to another word 37

time connective....a connecting word that helps sequence events in time 25

verb.........................a word or group of words that tells what is happening in a **clause**

action 9

relating 11

saying 16

sensing and thinking 22

tense 71